People Who Changed th

The Story Of

KARL MARX

200 Years After His Birth

By Rachel Basinger

Foreword by David Macgregor • Preface by Johan Fornäs

PEOPLE WHO CHANGED THE COURSE OF HISTORY: THE STORY OF KARL MARX 200 YEARS AFTER HIS BIRTH

Copyright © 2017 Atlantic Publishing Group, Inc.

1405 SW 6th Avenue • Ocala, Florida 34471 • Phone 800-814-1132 • Fax 352-622-1875
Website: www.atlantic-pub.com • Email: sales@atlantic-pub.com
SAN Number: 268-1250

Library of Congress Cataloging-in-Publication Data

Names: Basinger, Rachel, 1992– author.
Title: The story of Karl Marx 200 years after his birth / by Rachel Basinger
Other titles: At head of title: People tht changed the course of history
Description: Ocala, Florida : Atlantic Publishing Group, Inc., 2017. | Includes bibliographical references and index.
Identifiers: LCCN 2017046776 (print) | LCCN 2017048487 (ebook) | ISBN 9781620234181 (ebook) | ISBN 9781620234174 (pbk. : alk. paper) | ISBN 9781620234167 (hardcover : alk. paper) | ISBN 1620234173 (alk. paper)
Subjects: LCSH: Marx, Karl, 1818-1883. | Marx, Karl, 1818-1883—Philosophy. | Marx, Karl, 1818-1883—Influence. | Communism. | Socialism. | Marxian economics.
Classification: LCC HX45 (ebook) | LCC HX45 .B37 2017 (print) | DDC 335.4092 [B]—dc23

LC record available at https://lccn.loc.gov/2017046776

Printed in the United States

PROJECT MANAGER: Danielle Lieneman
INTERIOR LAYOUT AND JACKET DESIGN: Nicole Sturk

Reduce. Reuse.
RECYCLE.

A decade ago, Atlantic Publishing signed the Green Press Initiative. These guidelines promote environmentally friendly practices, such as using recycled stock and vegetable-based inks, avoiding waste, choosing energy-efficient resources, and promoting a no-pulping policy. We now use 100-percent recycled stock on all our books. The results: in one year, switching to post-consumer recycled stock saved 24 mature trees, 5,000 gallons of water, the equivalent of the total energy used for one home in a year, and the equivalent of the greenhouse gases from one car driven for a year.

Over the years, we have adopted a number of dogs from rescues and shelters. First there was Bear and after he passed, Ginger and Scout. Now, we have Kira, another rescue. They have brought immense joy and love not just into our lives, but into the lives of all who met them.

We want you to know a portion of the profits of this book will be donated in Bear, Ginger and Scout's memory to local animal shelters, parks, conservation organizations, and other individuals and nonprofit organizations in need of assistance.

– Douglas & Sherri Brown,
President & Vice-President of Atlantic Publishing

Dedication

To my parents, Gary and LaRue Basinger, for all the time they invested in my education and for teaching me how to love learning.

Table of Contents

FOREWORD
David Macgregor

In 1963, I discovered a thin volume of some of Karl Marx's writings in my high school library. Marx's magisterial survey of history and philosophy dazzled me. I was transfixed by his unique perspective that revealed human relations and political reality in a new light. The slender library book whisked me suddenly into Marx's fabled world, as Dorothy was whisked into Oz by the tornado. My parents were alarmed and puzzled by their teenage son's new devotion to the scary German communist. That chance meeting between Marx and me changed my life, just as Marx profoundly affected the lives of many millions of people.

200 years after his birth, Karl Marx remains a mystery. His ideas transformed the world in the years following his death in 1883. Marx's communist doctrine, largely assembled with generous financial assistance from his friend Friedrich Engels (himself a supremely wealthy capitalist), provided the leading ideas that forged the Russian Revolution of 1917. While communism has come and gone in Russia and the nations of Eastern Europe, Marx's revolutionary writings are still very much alive in China, North Korea, Vietnam, and Cuba. In India and other countries of the developing world, Karl Marx is a household name, and large communist parties are part of the political landscape.

And yet, Marx expected his ideas to take hold first in the countries of the West. In line with these hopes, Marxism formed a key part of the political turmoil in Europe that followed the Russian Revolution. Communist parties in Italy, France, and Germany constructed a fragile and temporary barrier against fascism. The communist ideal inspired opponents of Hitler in Russia and much of Europe during World War II, and Marx's legacy helped defeat the Nazis. Right up to the fall of the Soviet Union in 1991, Karl Marx's bitter denunciation of capitalism and his glowing dreams for a socialist future were shared by many in Western Europe. Even in America, Marx influenced political life during the 1930s and 1940s until the Cold War between the USSR and the United States shoved his ideas under a very dark and forbidding cloud.

Today we are in a new Cold War between America and Putin's Russia, but Marxism has little resonance in this subterranean conflict. Suspicions about China in the West admittedly have something to do with the country's communist rulers. However, much of China's wealth is in the hands of Red Capitalists, who resemble most of the rising 19th century capitalist class of Marx's time. China's growing influence in world trade and its astonishing industrial growth are more due to the fabulous success of Chinese entrepreneurship than to prescriptions drawn from the writings of Marx.

Although Marx's political influence has waxed and waned, his ideas still have an enormous grasp on the world imagination. Marx helped define the fundamental clash between workers and capitalists that remains a significant part of political and social life. Almost everywhere on the planet, governments composed of representatives of the capitalist class are very much in power. Industrial strife and exploitation of workers form a significant aspect of politics, just as Marx might have anticipated.

Marx had a high regard for the United States of America. He seriously considered immigrating to Texas during a rough period in his career. Imagine Marx in a cowboy hat, saddled on a bucking bronco! The German revolutionary's fondness for America is part of his enduring mystery. Marx suggested at times that the American example was much closer to his ideal of a communist future than the old regimes of Europe.

As Rachel Basinger shows in this wonderfully readable book, Marx in his time was best known as a journalist who contributed most of his work to American newspapers such as the New York Tribune. The American Civil War fascinated the bearded revolutionary, and, as leader of the International Working Men's Association, Marx even wrote to President Lincoln to congratulate him on his world historical opposition to slavery. No one outside the United States likely grieved the death of Abraham Lincoln more than the German communist who drafted his world-altering texts in London's British Museum Library.

Marx married a German aristocrat named Jenny von Westphalen and spent most of his life in England. His influential books on economics and politics almost totally overlooked the fact that the most powerful country in the world at the time, Great Britain, was governed by an oligarchy of royals and aristocrats, not capitalists. Britain to this day is an example of the old imperialist world of aristocracy and royal blood that dominated all of Europe in Marx's lifetime.

This is another part of the enduring mystery of Marx. While ignoring the aristocratic make-up of Great Britain, and downplaying England's cruel imperialist domination of most of the globe, Marx totally did not predict the astonishing late 19th-century rise of Germany, and the United States as formidable industrial competitors to the so-called British "workshop of the world."

And while Marx is rightly credited as an expert on revolution, he contributed practically nothing on the greatest revolution in world history that occurred in the New World after a little tea party in Boston. The American Revolution has hardly any place in anything Marx wrote. Perhaps it was because Marx, like many Germans of his time, identified completely with England and the British government, and ignored the fantastic uprising in America that defeated the world's most awe-inspiring military power and forever consigned aristocracy and royalty to the dustbin of history.

Marx constantly wrote under the shadow of the world-renowned German philosopher G.W.F. Hegel who died in 1831, when Marx was just 13 years old. As a teenager, Marx admitted that he was a student of Hegel, but he ultimately rejected many of the philosopher's ideas on democracy, freedom, and progress. Ironically, some of Marx's followers and friends immigrated to the United States where they fought on the Union side against the Confederacy. Many of these men distinguished themselves for valour and bravery during that terrible earth-shaking conflict when black and white Americans united to smash the grotesque institution of slavery.

After the Civil War ended, a few of these former German communists joined the Hegelian philosophical movement in Cincinnati and St. Louis, which significantly shaped the history of the United States in the late 19th and early 20th centuries. American Hegelianism inspired some of the Republic's greatest thinkers. Perhaps if Marx had immigrated to the New World, as he had planned to do several times during his life, he too might have ended up as an American Hegelian, and the history that we read about in Rachel Basinger's fascinating biography of Marx would never have happened.

 Karl Marx and G. W. (Wilhelm) F. Hegel will likely be bound together forever in the annals of political philosophy. In some ways similar, their outlook is also quite different as suggested by these two contradictory quotes.

Hegel: "The rational is actual and the actual is rational."

Marx: "The philosophers have only interpreted the world; the point however is to change it."

PREFACE
Johan Fornäs

Two centuries after his birth, Marx's rich work stands out among the great classics. He is still controversial as a political figure, but also as a materialist philosopher, a social historian, and not least the most famous founding father of capitalism critique.

Marx offered convincing explanations for lots of phenomena in modern life and society, which made it possible to see how different issues and phenomena are linked as parts of the same capitalist system. At the same time, he radiated a confidence in trusting one's own capacity for critical thinking rather than blindly believing in expert authorities. He identified key injustices of the social world, constructing an ingenious model to explain how they were established and why they are stubbornly reproduced, all while holding a door open for emancipatory social change.

Few others are equally famous or have similar places in history, combining deep involvement in political activism with qualified social theory and advanced philosophical reflection. This gives him a rather unique position in intellectual and political history.

Marx provided a key to understanding how all aspects of modern society are interconnected, from the high, lofty ideals to the low everyday futilities; from the global macro trends to the micro details of daily life; from global trade to consumerism; from common sense to religious beliefs; from technology to fashion; from economic history to the ecological crisis.

Moreover, his explanations uncover how capitalism is reproduced and how it survives, since its ordinary mechanisms produce illusions and false understandings and we, for instance, think that natural resources or machines can create value, or that we get fairly paid for our work. Marx thus criticizes the central bourgeois theories and ideologies, but equally much the capitalist practices that legitimate the exploitation and injustice that they hide behind a false aura of freedom and equality. He also communicates a sense in which this model of capitalist society is not fixed once and for all, but rather filled with internal contradictions that open up to change and action by each individual. His many unfinished writings make clear that they too deserve critical scrutiny and further development, as they just hint at fruitful directions for never-ending critical thought.

Marx's work is repeatedly declared to be outdated, as capitalism renews itself in ways that nobody in the 19th century could predict. However, with every new big crisis for capitalism, there is yet a revival, with new readers striving for fresh interpretations. For instance, in the 1920s and 30s, when the Great Depression gave rise to massive unemployment, personal catastrophes, and the disastrous rise of fascism, intellectuals formed a new understanding of contemporary culture and society in the 'Critical Theory' centered on Frankfurt in Germany, renewing traditional Marxism with inspiration from Freud's psychoanalysis as well as more recent philosophy and sociology.

Then, in the 1970s, the oil crisis fueled new social movements based on gender, sexuality, race, and ethnicity, but also a new generation of critical thought as the field of 'cultural studies' got a global dissemination. Finally, in this millennium, a series of deep financial collapses have again made people aware of the unreliability and unfairness of the world market and made young activists increasingly interested in taking part of the new readings of Marx's theory of capitalism.

Approaching his 200th birthday, the thoughts and writings of Marx remain refreshingly up-to-date and relevant not least to young people today. There is a special affinity between him and young people. He developed a kind of youthful thinking: critical, curious and committed, alert and ambitious, flexible and sharp. Also, by combining theoretical work with political activism, he opened up the intellectual ivory tower toward working class people and everyday experience. His texts invite readers to trust their own judgment, to stand up against those with inherited power and wealth, and to stand for equal rights and individual free development in solidarity with others. Marx therefore is suited best to those with young minds that question authority and open up to the world rather than those who prefer self-enclosed fundamentalist fortresses.

Marx's personal writing style was ruthlessly sharp but also elegant, learned, but often fun. He formulated lots of memorable one-liners, like "The philosophers have only *interpreted* the world, in various ways; the point, however, is to *change* it," "Religion is the opium of the people," "The history of all hitherto existing societies is the history of class struggles," and "The emancipation of the working classes must be conquered by the working classes themselves." His texts are full of witty satire and clever puns, but also of serious compassion and moving social reportage.

At the same time, Marx manages to deliver careful arguments and builds complex theories not just to cultivate a critical engagement, but also to carefully explain how capitalist societies can thrive. Combining all this, his lasting influence is backed by his unique grounding of the political and theoretical work on solid philosophical discourse, in dialogue with the best thinkers of his time.

Marx's motto, borrowed from the classical Roman author Terence, was, "Nothing human is alien to me," and this respect for humanity also invited his readers to learn from him to trust their own reason and to avoid the hubris of fanaticism. He is also famous for his formulation of socialist ethics: "From each according to his ability, to each according to his needs." This is one of those key ideals that continue to guide emancipatory efforts together with the so-called Golden Rule ("treat others how you wish to be treated") and Jesus' words in the Gospel of Mark ("love your neighbour as yourself").

Marx had a turbulent life in the interface between the most important current events and discourses of his time. He was at the same time both an engaged activist and a learned theorist, and this book also shows how he moved across Western Europe, communicating with friends and colleagues and always ready for critique, thus combining solidarity and independence in a striking way.

Marx took the best from German philosophy, French socialist politics, and British economic theory, scrutinized their inner contradictions and flaws, and constructed his own perspective on the industrial capitalism that was then being established on both sides of the Atlantic. Thereby he had a unique and lasting influence on philosophical reflection, leftist politics, and economic theory, leaving traces in all later critical movements in the social and intellectual fields: socialism and feminism, critical theory and cultural studies, civil rights movements, and postcolonial critique.

Marx was not dogmatic. His openness to the world was never uncritical, but this critique was no moralizing judgment. Instead, he always looked for inner contradiction in those texts and social relations that he approached. He thought that critique could only be effective if it really hit its target, and that demanded a deep understanding of that target. To attack capitalism where it hurt, he therefore had to find the deep-seated tensions and conflicts in that society, which made generous promises to its citizens and workers, but then betrayed them by denying them access to the welfare produced on the basis of wage labor.

In a letter from 1843, Marx declared, "We develop new principles for the world out of the world's own principles." And when reflecting on the lessons from the Paris Commune in 1871, he concluded that the working class has "no ideals to realize, but to set free the elements of the new society with which old collapsing bourgeois society itself is pregnant."

One should measure culture and society against its own ideal rather than putting an external ideal image against the existing social order. Hence, the trick is to make conscious the inner contradictions, tensions, conflicts, and ambivalences that crisscross today's world, and against the prevailing greedy exploitation and authoritarian injustices and find the emancipatory forces that are also born in this society and that may one day change the world.

Marx did not raise an abstract ideal and judge the present society from its failure to meet this ideal. Instead, he identified in society the emerging forces of emancipation and contrasted them to the many barriers and obstacles that stood against them. Today, with climate change and threatening ecological catastrophe, recurring financial crises and antidemocratic extreme nationalism thriving, this task of identifying and contrasting emancipating and barbarian potentials is as pertinent as ever.

In this spirit, Marx's work continues to inspire critical thinking and feeling, responding to the dynamic conditions of life in today's world.

INTRODUCTION
March 17, 1883

⋇} *"Before All Else a Revolutionist"* {⋇

On March 17, 1883, a date that you probably do not recognize, an Englishman commemorated the death of a man whom the Englishman called "the greatest living thinker." Only 11 people showed up for this funeral of a friend and family member. The man being eulogized had written several books, but none of them were best-sellers. He and his wife struggled to make ends meet throughout their lives. Four of his seven children died in infancy and childhood. The great political program that he helped shape never came to fruition during his lifetime. By any stretch of the imagination, we would all say that such a man was not successful. But within half a century of his death, his name became a household name, known throughout the world.

"The greatest living thinker" was Friedrich Engels' description of Karl Marx. Almost everyone in America recognizes Marx's name, or at the very least, an ideology called Marxism that is based on his name. We know that his idea of communism spread throughout Eastern Europe, Russia, and Asia in the 20th century and caused millions of deaths. But you probably do not know very much about the man behind Marxism.

According to Engels and later communists like Vladimir Lenin, Marx represented the epitome of mankind. Engels, in his eulogy at Marx's burial at Highgate Cemetery in London, heaps praise upon praise on the revolutionary (as people often do in eulogies), noting that Marx's death has created a gap for both the radical proletariat and history itself. Additionally, Engels makes the claim that Marx did for history what Charles Darwin did for science — a goal to which Marx always aspired throughout his life — and that Marx discovered how to solve the problems of capitalist society, which others had failed to do. Moreover, in every area that Marx investigated, he made an original discovery. In past ages, Engels observed, such a man might have been known as a man of science. But Marx went beyond such a category. He changed science into a revolutionary force. Thus, the highest compliment we can give Marx is that he was "before all else a revolutionist."[1]

Marx did for the proletariat what others refused to do. All types of governments, absolute to republic, and the bourgeoisie hated him. But Marx refused to give up. Consequently, he will be forever remembered: "And he died beloved, revered, and mourned by millions of revolutionary fellow workers — from the mines of Siberia to California, in all parts of Europe and America — and I make bold to say that, though he may have had many opponents, he had hardly one personal enemy. His name will endure through the ages, and so also will his work."[2]

While Engels, Marx's best friend, certainly was biased and likely to say the strongest statements about his friend, Engels's assessments have turned out to be correct. For good or for ill, Karl Marx will be forever remembered as the man who introduced communism to the world.

---

1. Engels, 1993.
2. Engels, 1993.

CHAPTER 1

Trier 1818-1836

⤨ *"Glowing Tears of Noble Men"* ⤧

The country we today call Germany did not acquire its name until 1871 with the end of the Franco-Prussian War and the Unification of Germany. Previously, Germany had been a confederation of 39 states (known as the German Confederation), including the more prominent regions of Prussia, Austria, Bavaria, Saxony, and Hanover. In 1867, the Northern German states consolidated under Prussian leadership in the North German Confederation. Several South German states remained independent Otto von Bismarck, chancellor of Prussia, combined these states into the German Empire in 1871.

Four decades after the United States of America was founded, during the presidency of James Monroe, 3,000 miles away in the Rhineland, an area in Germany (then Prussia) that touches France, Carl (Karl) Heinrich Marx was born on May 5, 1818 to Heinrich and Henriette Marx. Karl had six siblings who lived to adulthood: Sophie, Hermann, Henriette, Louise, Emilie, and Caroline. Tragically, two of his three brothers, Moritz David, the oldest child in the family, and Edward, the youngest child in the family, died before reaching their teenage years. Thus, Karl became the eldest son when his brother David died at four years old. His father, Heinrich (1777-1838), was from Saarlouis in Germany while Karl's mother, Henriette née Presburg (1788-1863), was from Nijmegen in the Netherlands and spoke Dutch.

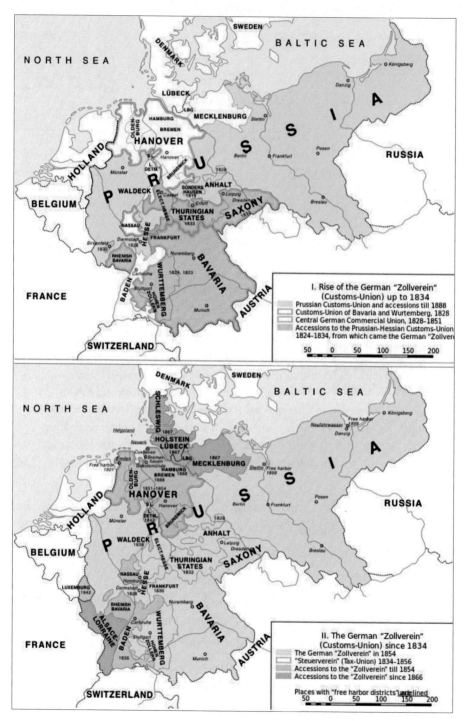

A map of the German Confederation.

When the two married in 1814, blessed by Henriette's substantial dowry (4,500 Prussian talers), Heinrich, then 37 years old, was 11 years older than his 26-year-old bride.[3] Interestingly, Henriette did not learn to speak German until the year she was to be married. Karl did not get along with or like his mother, but deeply respected his father, a successful lawyer who appreciated the Enlightenment, especially the writings of Immanuel Kant and Voltaire. In fact, Karl carried a picture of his father throughout his life (and was even buried with that picture).[4]

 Immanuel Kant was a German philosopher who lived from 1724 to 1804. He was one of the foremost thinkers of the Enlightenment and tried to reconcile the rationalism of René Descartes, which emphasized reason, and the empiricism of Francis Bacon, which emphasized experience. Kant is known for his comprehensive works in epistemology (the study of knowledge), ethics (the study of right and wrong actions), and aesthetics (the study of beauty), including *The Critique of Pure Reason*, *The Critique of Practical Reason*, and *The Critique of Judgment*.

The Marx family was well off. With an annual income of 1,500 talers (English thaler), the Marxs belonged in the top 5 percent of the city.[5] Of course, the family was not in league with bankers and property owners, but still had a significant income. In other words, Heinrich Marx earned three times the amount an actor, teacher, or baker would make and 15 times as much as a messenger, servant, or journeyman.[6] Because Germany was not a unified country until 1871, it is challenging to explain the exact value of the taler in the Rhineland in the 1810s, as every principality and state set the value of their currency differently. After the German Empire was founded in 1871, one taler would have equaled about 75 cents in the United States, meaning that the Heinrich's yearly income would have been

---

3. Sperber, 2013.
4. Callinicos, 2012.
5. Sperber, 2013.
6. "German Silver Coins."

around $1,125.[7] By contrast, an agricultural worker in the United States would have made around $300 in 1860.[8]

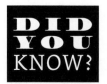 The taler underwent several changes as a currency. In 1566, the Reichthaler was installed as a uniform currency for trade. From then until the Napoleonic period, Prussia, Austria, and Bavaria reformed their currencies. Although Napoleon changed some coins, Prussia began a new currency reform after Napoleon was defeated at Waterloo, producing the Prussian taler, which the Marx family would have used. In northern Germany, the Prussian taler was the dominant currency. After the German Empire was founded in 1871, Germany adopted a single currency, the German mark, but the taler continued to be used for some time after.

Trier: Marx's hometown

Trier, the city into which Karl Marx was born, was an old Roman city. In fact, Trier had briefly served as the capital of the Western Roman Empire in the third century A.D. Trier also played an important role in the Middle Ages: it was the oldest seat of a bishop north of the Alps and held the Archbishop-Elector, one of the seven electors of the Holy Roman Empire. More recently, Trier had switched hands from Prussia to France several times. Trier had belonged to the Kingdom of Prussia until the French claimed Trier in 1794 during the French Revolutionary Wars. When the Napoleonic Wars ended in 1815, Trier returned to Prussia.

 In 17 B.C., the Roman Emperor Augustus founded the city "Augusta Treverorum," now known as Trier, likely making it the oldest city in modern-day Germany.[9] Trier was also one of the five largest cities in the Roman Empire with a population of 70,000 to 100,000 in the fourth century A.D. The famous Porta Nigra ("Black Gate"), a large Roman city gate, was built from 186 to 200 A.D.

---

7. "German Silver Coins."
8. Wright, 1889.
9. "Trier: The Center of Antiquity in Germany," 2012.

Trier, Karl Marx's birthplace.

Porta Nigra, a large Roman city gate.

In contrast to the rest of Germany, which was strongly Protestant after the Reformation in the 1500s, Trier was an extremely Catholic city. Protestants and Jews were in the substantial minority. Although Jews had to pay extra taxes, they still could hold high positions in the city. On August 8, 1794, the French revolutionaries took control of Trier. Three years later in 1797, Trier and the entire Rhineland were integrated into the French state. The French revolutionaries requested 1.5 million livres from the city, and, in 1823, five years after Karl Marx was born, Trier still owed 56,000 Prussian talers (or roughly $42,000).[10]

 Napoleon Bonaparte (1769-1821) is an extremely recognized figure who belongs among the most prominent people in the history of the Western World along with Alexander the Great and Julius Caesar. Known as the Corsican or the Little Corporal, Napoleon was the most famous French general and later emperor. He is known for his intense desire for the military expansion of France, his disastrous Russian campaign of 1812 — famously depicted in a graphic by Charles Joseph Minard — and the Napoleonic Code. But you may not know that although Napoleon was only 5'6", that was the average height for a man in the 1800s. You also may not know that George Orwell used Napoleon's iconic name in *Animal Farm*, a fairy story about the Russian Revolution, perhaps inspiring the French law that forbids people from naming their pigs Napoleon![11] Finally, while there are several famous "Hundred Day" campaigns, including the Allied offensives in World War I during the fall of 1918, Napoleon's return to power after his exile on Elba is the most famous Hundred Day campaign.

When Napoleon became the first Emperor of the French, he tried to reconcile Trier and other Western German cities to French rule, and it appeared that he succeeded. During his tour of Trier and other cities in now eastern France, Napoleon received a big welcome in 1804.[12] When Napoleon was defeated at Waterloo on June 18, 1815, the Congress of Vienna, the peace settlement conference for the Napoleonic Wars, gave Trier back to Prussia.

---

10. Sperber, 2013.
11. Inge, 2015.
12. Sperber, 2013.

Because Trier and the Rhineland had experienced French liberties during the 21 years of French control, they came to resent Prussian authoritarianism. Alsace-Lorraine, which also switched hands several times during the 19th and 20th centuries, also disliked Prussia's strong hand.

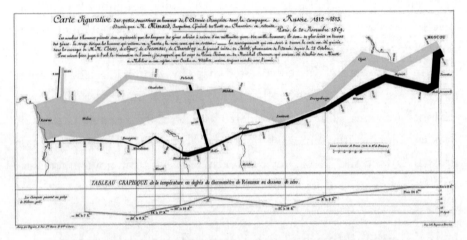

A map of Napoleon's Russian campaign of 1812 made by Charles Minard.

Although many people know that Napoleon was defeated at Waterloo and sent to St. Helena, 1,200 miles of the coast of Africa, in exile, they do not know much about the Congress of Vienna (1814-1815), an assembly that reorganized Europe after the Napoleonic Wars. Austria, Prussia, Russia, and Great Britain guided the discussion, although all former belligerents could send representatives. The Congress had two goals: establish a new balance of power and maintain the status quo. In other words, the territory changes that the Congress made were to ensure that no one country was too strong. The borders determined by the Congress stayed the same for 40 years (with minor exceptions) and Europe did not see another European-wide war until World War I. Before the Second World War, many viewed the Congress of Vienna as too weak and not successful in bringing about peace. Of course, Articles 231 and 232 of the Treaty of Versailles (which ended World War I) that established German war guilt and reparations would later receive much more condemnation after the Second World War. In hindsight, the Congress of Vienna was quite successful. There was not a major war until the Crimean War of 1854-1856, 40 years after the treaties were signed. Additionally, Europe maintained the status quo of conservatism (not the same as Republicans today) and traditionalism until the revolutions of 1848.

The people had several complaints against the Prussians: The Prussians were not Catholic, like almost everyone who resided in Trier; they raised already high taxes; and they seemed much more harsh than the French. Nonetheless, there was still some hope for the Jews of Trier. Before the Prussians reacquired the city, Prussia chancellor Prince von Hardenberg had issued The Edict of Emancipation of 1812 all throughout Prussia that gave Jews freedom of residence and occupation, with the potential exception of government officials and other public services, and the ability to serve in the military.[13] The edict stated that Jews who had fixed surnames and who used German "or another living language" in non-religious professional activities would be considered as natives and as state citizens of Prussia, enjoying "the same civil rights and liberties as Christians."[14] Later Prussian laws in the 1810s, however, excluded Jews from government service, including private attorneys like Heinrich Marx.[15]

Marx's Jewish Heritage and Later Protestant Background

Some historians point out the unfortunate coincidence and inconsistency that although Karl Marx was born a Jew, anti-Semitic (someone who is hostile to or prejudiced against Jews) leaders later utilized his ideas of socialism and communism. This topic is extremely nuanced. First, the word and concept of "totalitarianism" is often used to include fascism, Nazism, communism, and socialism. In fact, totalitarian refers to how much control the government has, which tends to be large in all of these ideologies. Second, people can assume that these ideologies are roughly the same, calling Adolf Hitler a fascist or Josef Stalin a socialist. Again, this is somewhat sloppy thinking. Fascism is a specific belief that emphasizes the importance of the state while Nazism focuses on nationalism (patriotic feelings toward one's country). Likewise, socialism is a broad category (as Marx himself

---

13. Sperber, 2013.
14. Levy.
15. Sperber, 2013.

noted in *The Communist Manifesto*), and communism is a subset of socialism. Although Stalin and Hitler both killed millions of people, they differed in political opinions. Hitler did not agree with Marx's beliefs and actually conflated Jews with Bolsheviks (Communists) and argued for the killing of both Jews and Communists. The Russian Communists like Stalin, however, were not Jewish, and the U.S.S.R. was an atheistic government. The Jews that were a part of the Soviet government were secular, and they focused on being dedicated Communists and abandoned their faith. Thus, there were very few Communist Jews. Additionally, the Soviets largely purged Jews from the government in Poland and other Eastern European countries after a while. All this to say Karl Marx might have had a place in Stalin's Soviet government, but as a secular Jew. His Jewishness would not have kept him out, but it would not have kept him in either.

Types of Socialism

Anarchism
(Advocates for self-governed societies often without states)

Communism
(Advocates for common ownership of the means of production)

Democratic Socialism
(Advocates for social ownership of the means of production as well as political democracy)

Maoism
(Advocates for a communist society led by peasants in China)

Religious Socialism
(Advocates for socialism based on religious principles)

Stalinism
(Advocates for the communist policies of Stalin, such as rapid industrialization and a centralized state)

Utopian Socialism
(Advocates for futuristic ideal societies)

The Marx family, however, was defined by their Jewishness, at least until Heinrich Marx converted to Protestantism in the 1810s. Although one of Karl's famous works was entitled *The Jewish Question*, Karl did not often invoke his Jewish heritage. Interestingly, Karl's daughter Eleanor Marx seems to have rediscovered her Jewish heritage later in life as she famously would begin her speeches in the late 1800s with, "I am a Jewess." Eleanor also learned Yiddish in her 30s and responded to an invitation to an event in October 1890 regarding the persecution of Jews in Russia with "Dear Comrade, I shall be very glad to speak at the meeting ... the more glad, that my father was a Jew."[16] More correctly, her ancestors were Jews in the sense that Marx's paternal relatives were Trier rabbis. His grandfather (Mordechai or Marx Lewry) was from Postolprti in Bohemia and became a rabbi in Saarlouis, a town near Trier.

In Napoleonic France of 1804 to 1814, Napoleon decreed that Jews would have to conform to social codes, including using family names, not patronymics, meaning that Jews would not use names derived from their fathers. Some Jews who lived in the country protested this law and refused to change their names, but many of the small population of Jews in Trier willingly altered their names, including Marx's relatives. Samuel Marx, a Trier rabbi who was Karl's uncle, took Marx as a surname to cooperate with this law, and the family followed suit.

 Patronymic means a name that is derived from the name of a father or another male ancestor, normally with the addition of a prefix or suffix. Patronymics are frequently used in Russia. For example, Aleksandr Solzhenitsyn's famous *One Day in the Life of Ivan Denisovich* includes a patronymic: Denisovich, which literally means "son of Denis."

---

16. Virdee, 2017.

Before Karl's father Heinrich became a lawyer, he had served as Trier Consistory secretary and perhaps left due to the salary.[17] Heinrich then moved to Osnabrück in lower Saxony so that Heinrich could work as a court translator. He wanted to work as a notary (a person who is authorized to perform certain legal functions, such as drawing up contracts or deeds), but was not allowed because he did not have domicile, or residency, status in Osnabrück. Perhaps due to his lack of success in becoming a notary, Heinrich opted to study law in Koblenz, which would discuss, among other topics, the Roman law. When Heinrich completed the program, he would be granted a certificate. Heinrich was the very last student to study at the School of Law in Koblenz as the Prussian military success brought the Napoleonic French rule in the Rhineland to an end.[18]

As noted above, the Edict of Emancipation, while beneficial to Jews in some respects, did restrict Heinrich from becoming an attorney as a Jew. He had two options: he could either select a different occupation or he could convert to Christianity, either Protestantism or Catholicism, which was significantly more prominent than the former. Heinrich decided to convert to Protestantism sometime in the 1810s, likely in 1819, and was baptized.[19] Karl was likely baptized five years later in 1824, and Henriette was not baptized until 1825 when both her parents died. While Heinrich's Protestantism opened doors for him professionally, he still remained in the minority. In a city of roughly 15,000 in the 1800s, Trier boasted of probably 200 Protestants, meaning that Heinrich was in the 1 percent.[20]

17. Sperber, 2013.
18. Sperber, 2013.
19. Sperber, 2013.
20. Sperber, 2013.

 Today when someone converts to another religion, he or she often feels that the new religion better explains life than a previous religion. Thus, conversion happens today due to beliefs. In the 1800s, conversion often happened for practical motives, not for doctrinal reasons. In Eastern Europe and Russia, Jews tended to convert more frequently when the regions experienced times of crisis and less often when regimes discussed ideas like emancipation and reform (like the Edict of Emancipation of 1812). According to the Yivo Encyclopedia of Jews in Eastern Europe, "[a] pattern was especially evident among the most affluent Jews, who had higher hopes for emancipation, and who had the most to lose when such hopes failed."[21] It is likely that Heinrich Marx would have fit into this category because early in the 1810s, there was a chance that he could serve as attorney as a Jew. But that changed in the late 1810s and Heinrich converted in order to work as a lawyer.

But Protestantism suited Heinrich better. He was a rationalist and follower of the Enlightenment. In addition to his penchant for Kant and Voltaire, Heinrich loved reading Leibnitz, Locke, and Newton and participated as a member in the Trier Casino Club, which was a liberal literary society. Christianity in the 19th century looked different from Christianity in previous centuries. Due to evangelical revivals in some largely Protestant countries, namely Britain and especially Germany, modern Biblical scholarship changed individuals' understandings of the Bible. One result was liberal theology, or the acceptance of Enlightenment ideas in Christian theology. In particular, the 19th century saw the rise of Biblical criticism, especially through the works of Friedrich Schleiermacher. In previous ages, the Bible had been considered the infallible Word of God, meaning there were no errors and cannot be wrong. With Biblical criticism, the Bible was viewed as an ordinary piece of literature that could be discussed and debated like the *Iliad*, Francis Bacon's *Novum Organon*, or any popular work of the day. This act placed the Bible on the same level as any other book and allowed individuals to look at the text (the who, where, when, why) and began to be used in anthropology, history, and religious studies.

---

21. Teter, 2010.

 Today in America, we tend to associate conservatism with gun-touting, Bible-thumping Republicans and liberalism with multicultural, socialist Democrats. In the 1800s, conservative and liberal meant something very different. Conservatism was a political philosophy that favors tradition, both religious and cultural, and was critical of proposals for radical social change (like socialism, communism, etc.) Specifically, conservatism eschewed (shunned) violent overthrows of government like the French Revolution of 1789, emphasized monarchy, aristocracy, and the church, favored obedience to political authority, desired balance of power, and wanted less freedom of the press, which was a liberal idea. Prominent 19th century conservatives include Austrian Klemens von Metternich, British Edmund Burke, French De Maistre, who was in favor of ultramontanism ("beyond the mountains"), meaning that the pope was the basis not only of the Catholic religion but also of all social order. Liberalism, by contrast, was an ideology that was based on the belief that people should be as free from restraint as possible. As one of my former students, David, described, conservatism set up barriers and walls while liberalism tried to tear them down. Liberalism owed much to the Enlightenment and the French Revolution, emphasized revolutionary, sometimes violent actions, preferred representative governments (and governments with written constitutions), promoted the sanctity of individuals, and believed that governments should protect natural rights and encourage equality of opportunity. Liberalism had two variants: economic liberalism, which focused on supply and demand and was also known as classic economics, and political liberalism, which argued that government should defend the country, protect individuals with police, and construct and maintain public works too expensive for individuals. Adam Smith, known for his famous work *The Wealth of Nations*, represented the former, and John Stuart Mill, who wrote *On Liberty* (1859), embodied the latter.

As many European nations experienced revolutions of many varieties from the French Revolution to the American Revolution (although one could argue that this event is better described as the War for Independence because revolution had a more violent connotation) to the Industrial Revolution, educated people throughout the continent, and especially in Germany, discussed the best way to handle all these changes. Heinrich Marx, as an Enlightenment man and newly baptized Protestant, would have leaned toward liberalism, rather than conservatism. Karl certainly took after his father as his works would regularly encouraged revolutionary and violent actions and encourage equality of opportunity.

Marx's Education

It is likely that Karl did not attend elementary school, but instead had private lessons at home, including writing lessons from Eduard Montigny, a Trier book dealer.[22] In 1830, Marx began attending the Trier Gymnasium (known as the Friedrich-Wilhelm-Gymnasium since 1896), which was a university-preparatory school. The Gymnasium focused on the classics, meaning works written in Latin and Greek (like Homer's *Iliad* and *Odyssey* and Virgil's *Aeneid*). Throughout his life, Marx used Greek and Latin phrases and referenced the classics. Additionally, Marx would use techniques he had learned in the Gymnasium in his later life. Given that the city of Trier was predominantly Catholic, it is no surprise that the school was 80 percent Catholic.[23]

As you probably have ascertained (realized), a Gymnasium in Germany in the 1800s is quite different from a gymnasium in the modern world! A Gymnasium (often with a capital letter) in early modern Germany was a state-maintained secondary school designed to prepare students for higher academic education in universities. Originating in Strassburg in 1537, a student would normally enter at age 12 or 13 and leave after age 16, often at 19 or 20. In modern terms, it would be similar to an extremely academically rigorous high school where all the students expected to go to university. Of course, it is important to remember that university attendance was much less common in the 1800s than it is today. The German Gymnasium had three main types, which differed based on curriculum: classical (Latin, Greek, and one modern language), modern (Latin and two modern languages), and mathematical and scientific (two spoken languages and optional Latin).[24]

---

22. Sperber, 2013.
23. McLellan, 2006.
24. "Gymnasium," 1998.

When Marx graduated in 1835, he was one of the youngest members of the class at 17. He belonged in the top fourth of the class, being eighth equal out of 32 students. His Latin and Greek grades were his best subjects, while mathematics and French were his weakest. In German, his work was very good, and he was reasonably proficient in religion and history. As the certificate of matriculation from 1835 states, "He has good abilities; he showed very satisfactory application in classical languages, in German and in history, satisfactory application in mathematics and only some application in French."[25]

Because Marx chose French, not Hebrew, as his third language, he indicated that he intended to pursue a career in law. If Marx had desired to join the clergy, he would have selected Hebrew.

Three of Marx's graduating exams have survived, including an essay for Latin about Augustus Caesar, one for Religion about John 15:1-14 (the vine and branches passage), and one for German, which discussed career choices. In his Religion essay, he showed his rationalist and Enlightenment tendencies, stating that Christianity was necessary for the full development of human beings, but not discussing Christ's redemptive work very much.

For his German essay, Marx suggested that while one could ask parents for advice about career choices, it was best to make one's own decisions. According to Marx, one should select an occupation that grants dignity to other human beings. As Marx himself stated, "When we have chosen the vocation in which we can contribute most to humanity, burdens cannot bend us because they are only sacrifices for all. Then we experience no meager, limited, egotistic joy, but our happiness belongs to millions, our deeds live on quietly but eternally effective, and glowing tears of noble men will

---

25. Kamenka, 1983.

fall on our ashes."[26] This essay, which illuminates the influence of the Kantian ideals of Johann Heinrich Wyttenbach and the Romanticism of literary giant Johann Wolfgang von Goethe, gave examples of individual accomplishments: scholar, sage, and poet. Interestingly, Marx did not list soldiers or lawyers.[27]

 Marx referenced characters, events, and themes from classical literature and the ancient world throughout his life. Faced with financial difficulties in the early 1860s, Marx stayed sane in early 1861 by reading the classics. Both Appian's *The Civil Wars* and Thucydides's *Histories* kept Marx relatively upbeat. But Marx did not view all those who lived in antiquity equally; he loved Spartacus, a slave who rose up against Rome from 73-71 B.C. ("the finest fellow produced by the whole of classical history ... a real representative of the ancient proletariat") while he despised Pompey, known for his extravagant wealth ("a pure louse of a man").[28] In another example, Marx mourned the death of Ferdinand Lassalle, a man who promoted international-style socialism in Germany in the mid-1800s, to a mutual friend, Countess Sophie von Hatzfeldt. While Marx and Lassalle had not always seen eye-to-eye (in fact, Marx once accused Lassalle of stealing ideas from *The Communist Manifesto*), Marx encouraged the countess to take joy in one aspect of Lassalle's untimely death in an 1864 duel: "He died young, in triumph, like Achilles [the great Greek fighter who killed untold numbers of Trojans and was virtually invincible, except for his heel]."[29]

26. Easton and Guddat, 1997.
27. Sperber, 2013.
28. McLellan, 2006.
29. McLellan, 2006.

CHAPTER 2
Bonn and Berlin 1836-1842

⊰ *"Studying Industriously and Attentively"* ⊱

Marx: The University Student

From the Trier Gymnasium, Marx moved onto the University of Bonn to study law. Although Marx intended to be there longer, his duration in Bonn only lasted one year due to personal difficulties. Founded in 1818, the University of Bonn included Rhenish (from the Rhineland) students and Prussian noblemen: "youths belonging to some of the highest and most ancient families in Germany are now receiving their academical education on the left bank of the Lower Rhine."[30] In the estimation of Englishman J.W. Parker writing in 1845, University of Bonn was the highest regarded and "numerously frequented" university in Germany, with the exception of the University of Berlin.[31] While Marx had some issues with drinking (not too much of a surprise since he was only 17 years old), he did not incur the wrath of his father until Marx participated in a duel in the summer of 1836. Not an ordinary duel when one man fought another over personal honor, Marx had attempted to defend Rhenish honor against

---

30. Parker, 1845.
31. Parker, 1845.

Prussian aristocrats.[32] As the University of Bonn reported in its record of studies for Marx, he was studying jurisprudence "industriously and attentively," but as "far as his conduct is concerned, it should be noted that he was sentenced to one day's imprisonment for drunkenness and causing a disturbance at night ..."[33]

Heinrich Marx, however, was not impressed and sent Karl a letter stating that he had high hopes for his son and that currently Karl was veering off course, even with his financial accounts. According to Heinrich, they were not orderly: "One demands order of a scholar, especially of a practical jurist."[34] Heinrich believed that a change of scenery would be the best course of action for Karl and required his son to go to the University of Berlin, the most prominent university in Germany.

The University of Bonn and the University of Berlin had some similarities: both were part of a group of Prussian universities founded by Frederick William III and both were research universities focused on developing a specialization for each individual. Additionally, they were both highly regarded. They differed mostly in location. Bonn was a small university town of 15,000 in the Rhineland, currently under Prussian jurisdiction but which France had previously occupied.[35] Berlin, by contrast, was a large city with a population of over 300,000, belonging among the great cities of London, Paris, Vienna, Rome, Madrid, and New York.[36] Additionally, Berlin was in the heart of Prussia and was the Prussian capital, giving it a different culture from Bonn. Finally, Berlin was 450 miles away from the Marx home in Trier whereas Bonn was only 100 miles away.

---

32. Sperber, 2013.
33. Kamenka, 1983.
34. Sperber, 2013.
35. Sperber, 2013.
36. Sperber, 2013.

The German research university, which first developed the concept of a Ph.D., grew out of the creation of the University of Berlin in 1811. In contrast to the liberal arts education of the Middle Ages and Renaissance, it was a new kind of university. The German research university wanted to develop the highest potential of an individual (which sounds like Marx in his German essay at the Gymnasium). One could pursue formation through specialization, embodied by the Ph.D. The faculty at a research university was there to teach you about yourself, and the professors are not instructors, but rather specialists. The *telos* (goal) of a German university was to engender culture, and a student learned knowledge as a fellow researcher.

Before Karl went to Berlin, he got engaged to a women four years his senior named Jenny Westphalen in the summer of 1836. Marx had grown up with Jenny and went to school with her brother. Jenny was known as the "prettiest girl in Trier" and the "queen of the ball."[37] Dr. Sperber has suggested that Marx's desire to marry an older woman in a society that scorned such behavior as scandalous may have been Marx's first act of rebellion.[38] In the end, Marx and Jenny were engaged for seven years, and their engagement was most epistolary, meaning that often they were apart from one another and had to write letters. Although Jenny's family had second-rate noble status (meaning that the family had recently acquired nobility, which occurred in the 1700s), Jenny would not have a substantial dowry because her father had already run through the family money. Originally, only Karl's parents knew about the engagement; Heinrich was happy, but Henriette was not. Later Karl and Jenny told Jenny's parents, Ludwig and Caroline von Westphalen, and both parents were pleased, especially Jenny's father who had been a mentor to Marx. Even so, like most fathers, Ludwig Westphalen expected Marx to have a job before they married. Since Marx planned to attend the University of Berlin in the fall, it would be a while before Karl and Jenny could marry, which Jenny (although older) accepted and waited patiently.

---

37. Sperber, 2013.
38. Sperber, 2013.

The University of Berlin, a university that Marx attended.

Thus, Jenny stayed in Trier, and Karl traveled 450 miles to Berlin to attend the renowned University of Berlin. At the university, Marx encountered the writings of a philosopher who would influence Marx throughout his entire life: Georg Wilhelm Friedrich Hegel. Just as Kant's opinions had shaped Heinrich Marx's beliefs, Hegel's philosophy would guide Karl Marx's ideas. As one of the interesting coincidences in history, Hegel took the chair of philosophy at University of Berlin in 1818, the same year Marx was born. Unfortunately for Marx, Hegel died in 1831, five years before Marx would attend the university. Hegel's influence, however, was still felt throughout the university.

Friedrich Hegel with some of his Berlin students.

While Karl Marx is likely the most prominent attendee of the University of Berlin, both Søren Kierkegaard and Jakob Burckhardt are names and people you should know. Kierkegaard was a Danish philosopher who was a Christian existentialist known as the "father of existentialism." Existentialism focuses on humans, especially suffering, and emphasizes the free will of individuals. Friedrich Nietzsche, Martin Heidegger, and Jean-Paul Sartre were other famous existentialists. Albert Camus is often considered an existentialist, but he did not consider himself one. *Fear and Trembling*, which is Kierkegaard's definitive work, illustrates the last of Kierkegaard's three stages of aesthetic, ethical, and religious (which requires a leap of faith). Jakob Burckhardt was a Swiss historian of art and culture who also discussed historiography. In "On Fortune and Misfortune in History," Burckhardt stresses that there are limits of history. Because human beings are in the middle of things, a historian cannot determine origins or endings. A historian (and normal individuals observing history) has to be able to say, "I don't know." Human beings cannot know what history is doing. Although raised in a Protestant household, Burckhardt later abandoned his Christian faith, but always had a profound respect for the end fate of man.

Two faculty members in particular captivated Marx: Savigny in jurisprudence and Gans in criminal law.[39] While Savigny impressed Marx with his historical knowledge and argumentation skills, Gans was certainly more influential. Gans had observed French socialists and may have been Marx's adviser for his dissertation had the former not died of a stroke in 1839. Even so, Gans made his mark. Many passages from *The Communist Manifesto* resemble works by Gans (some are almost verbatium).[40] Marx stopped attending juridical classes, but he studied industriously.

The Young Hegelians

In the summer of 1837, less than a year after Marx arrived in Berlin, Marx encountered another prominent influence that would guide him the rest of his life: the Young Hegelians. They were called "young" because they liked the French Revolution of 1789 and wanted to apply its success to future revolutions. Some, like Italian Giuseppe Mazzini, whose work would later lead to Italian Unification in 1871, named his politically radical society, "Young Italy." In Germany, Heinrich Heine would use the name, "Young Germany" for a literary movement. At first, the Young Hegelians used Hegelian dialectic in religion; then they moved to politics and developed Higher Criticism. When Prussian monarch Friedrich Wilhelm IV ascended the throne in 1840, the Young Hegelians moved more to the left through democratic and republican ideals.

39. Stapley, 2010.
40. Sperber, 2013.

Monarch Friedrich Wilhelm IV of Prussia.

 Georg Wilhelm Friedrich Hegel (1770-1831) is one of the most influential thinkers in the Western World. Regularly mentioned and discussed by educated individuals from the 1800s to present, Hegel embodied German idealist philosophy. He argued that his system of philosophy was a culmination of previous philosophical thought. In particular, Hegel responded to and critiqued the ideas of Immanuel Kant, a philosopher who had tried to bring together rationalism (which focused on reason) and empiricism (which focused on the senses). Hegel had a complex way to understand history. He believed that the ultimate goal of history is reason and that all progress in history has pointed toward this goal. Like Hegel, later philosophers (like the Young Hegelians) would use this idea of progress even if they came to different conclusions. Hegel believed that individuals are alienated (separated) from the Absolute Spirit of Reason, but that as individuals become more self-conscious (or self-aware), they will understand increasingly more the Absolute Spirit of Reason. Hegel believed that self-consciousness was the way for humans to fully develop.

After the death of their idol, the Young Hegelians combined Hegel's theology with rationalist ideas, known today as Higher Criticism (investigating the origins of ancient texts in order to understand "the world behind the text" as opposed to Lower Criticism, which is looking at the text itself). Three individuals who not only defined the movement but also made a substantial impact on Marx were David Strauss, Ludwig Feuerbach, and Bruno Bauer.

 Young Italy helped to unify Italy! A political movement for Italian youth (not just teens ... you could be up to 40 years old!) founded in 1831 by Giuseppe Mazzini, Young Italy wanted to create a united Italian republic. By attracting many Italians to the cause of independence, it assisted in the Risorgimento (struggle for Italian unification). Believing that violence and revolution was the road to independence, the influence of Mazzini's Young Italy waned, and the Piedmont began to lead the Risorgimento in 1850. Italy would finally unify in 1871, interestingly the same year when Germany unified. One unique aspect about Young Italy is that they wore red shirts.

UNIONE, FORZA E LIBERTA!!

A Young Italy political movement flag.

One of the first Young Hegelians to discuss theological topics, David Strauss appears to have a more generic influence on Marx. Nonetheless, Strauss demonstrated his radical thoughts in *Life of Jesus Theologically Examined*, published in 1835, which stated that the gospel stories were merely projections of the Jews and that Jesus' life could not be verified empirically.

Ludwig Feuerbach made a similar claim in *Essence of Christianity* (1841), arguing that humans attribute their best aspects to a mythical supernatural being. While Marx read Feuerbach's works, they never met and Feuerbach distanced himself from Marx. Nonetheless in 1845, Marx wrote a short work entitled "Theses on Feuerbach," which were published posthumously in 1888 by Friedrich Engels. The theses, however, argued that Feuerbach in desiring to remove religious beliefs from the social sphere had not gone far enough. Rather, Marx posited that the root issue, namely the social and economic structure, needed to be reformed.

Bruno Bauer, by far one of the most significant (and sometimes overlooked) influences on Marx, argued against the traditional view that Jesus was the Son of God and instead suggested that individuals who were religious took the Jewish myths about Jesus and transformed them in their human self-consciousness. Bauer laid out these ideas predominantly in two books: *Critique of the Gospel of John* (1840) and *Critique of the Synoptic Gospels* (1841). Bauer and Marx corresponded, and Marx looked up to Bauer as a mentor and adviser. Bauer wanted Marx to join him at the University of Bonn as a professor, but Bauer's liberal and antireligious ideas got him kicked out, leaving Marx with no university professorships. Bauer also critiqued Strauss's ideas and became anti-Semitic.

Bruno Bauer, one of Marx's greatest influences.

The word "synoptic" means general in view, or a common vision. The gospels of Matthew, Mark, and Luke are known as the Synoptic Gospels because they include many of the same stories, covering many of the same events of Jesus' life in a similar order. Nearly 90 percent of Mark's content is found in Matthew, and about 50 percent of Mark appears in Luke. Parables are found in all of the Synoptic Gospels while the Gospel of John includes no parables. In fact, every story or parable found in Mark is found in Matthew and Luke. Yet there are also major differences in the three Synoptic Gospels, leading to the so-called "Synoptic Problem," in which a variety of scholars attempt to address how the three gospels include much of the same material, yet still differ in content, wording, and order.

In a letter to his father in November 1837, Marx revealed the deep influence Hegel and the Young Hegelians had played in his life, invoking the historical progress of Hegel's Spirit. Again, Heinrich Marx was unimpressed by Marx's letter and again chided his son for lack of progress and development and for squandering family money. While Heinrich did not mandate a university change this time, he did insist that Karl return home on the Easter recess of 1838, which Karl did.[41] When Karl journeyed home that Easter, he found his father dying (Heinrich did die soon thereafter on May 10, 1838). Karl also got into a quarrel with Jenny after a year and a half of not seeing her. When Marx left Trier on May 7, 1838, he would not return home for the rest of his time at University of Berlin. To make matters worse, with his father's death, Marx could no longer afford his studies at the university, which would certainly impact his relationship with Jenny (already tenuous due to the fight they had over Easter). Marx requested that his mother, with whom he had a tense relationship with, send money for university fees and living expenses. The Westphalen family had snubbed Henriette by not making a condolence call after her husband's death, so Henriette knew that she would be perpetuating Karl's engagement with Jenny.[42] Even so, Karl did eventually receive enough funds to finish at the university.

---

41. Sperber, 2013.
42. Sperber, 2013.

 Leucippus and his student Democritus, who was known as the "laughing philosopher" for his emphasis on the importance of cheerfulness, first proposed Atomism. Atomists like Democritus argued that atoms are the smallest indivisible bodies from which everything else is composed and that they move in an infinite void. Atomism is a materialist (meaning matter is all there is and no spiritual forces exist) and determinist (meaning every human action is inevitable) view of the world.

Marx's Doctoral Dissertation

Now financially equipped, Marx began work on his doctoral dissertation so that he could join Bauer at the University of Bonn (a hope unrealized because Bauer lost his position as mentioned above). The topic of Marx's dissertation was a comparison of the theories of nature in two ancient Greek atomists, Democritus and Epicurus. Contrary to popular opinion of the day, Marx argued that Epicurus went beyond Democritus and had the more original theory of atomism (the theory that all reality and objects in the universe are composed of small indivisible building blocks known as atoms from the Greek "atomos," meaning uncuttable). Marx's dissertation showed the clear influence of Hegel and the Young Hegelians as it contained the Hegelian progressive development. Marx preferred Epicurus's ideas because they were at a higher stage of self-consciousness than those of Democritus. From the body of the dissertation, Marx demonstrated the major influence Hegel had on Marx's philosophy and beliefs.

Democritus	Epicurus
Believed atoms moved, but did not explain why	Believed that atoms moved downward and added another tendency: the swerve (occasionally and randomly atoms will move to one side)
Believed that only atoms and the void existed and that qualities from the senses (like color, taste, etc.) came only from convention	Believed that atoms and qualities from the senses existed and were real

The preface and introduction were also revealing. In the preface, Marx quoted Prometheus, a Titan in Greek mythology who stole fire from Mount Olympus and gave it to mankind: "[W]ith a word, I hate each and every god." Marx then expounded that this statement belongs to philosophy and that there shall be no other god besides human self-consciousness. With this retort, Marx indicated that he was moving beyond the Ten Commandments of the Old Testament as the first commandment given by Jehovah is, "You shall have no other gods before me." Marx's statement that human self-consciousness was the highest divinity reveals that he intended to replace the Hebrew and Christian God with philosophy and Hegelian dialectic.

Although the word "atomism" or the name Epicurus may not be familiar, you probably know more about them than you think! Epicurus was an ancient Greek who sought to avoid pain, advocated for materialism (only matter exists, nothing spiritual), and argued against the existence of a deity. Current sentiment connects Epicureanism to modern science, stating that science has "point by point" (in Nietzsche's words) proved Christianity false and Epicureanism (an ancient philosophy that preferred mental pleasure to pain) correct.[43] Even though modern science and Epicureanism share the goal of liberating the world from irrational belief, today's scientists and yesterday's Epicureans stud-

---

43. Nietzsche, 1995.

ied the natural world in very different ways. Epicurus had no real scientific curiosity. Instead, he wanted to release humanity from matter and the gods. He desired freedom, not truth. By contrast, other Greek philosophers (who incidentally were pagans), such as Socrates, Plato, and Aristotle, did not support Epicurus's materialism. In fact, they held views that align more closely with modern science than Epicureanism.

A bust of Epicurus, a Greek philosopher.

Although Marx had completed most of his university work at the University of Berlin, he could not submit his thesis to the university because he had not applied for an extension past the normal four years. Because Marx had matriculated in 1836, he had to submit his thesis by 1840. Marx was a year late, and, as a result, had to submit his dissertation to the University of Jena instead. The University of Jena was the only German university that did not require a defense or residency, but was still a reputable university. In a letter, Dr. Carl Friedrich Bachmann, Dean of the Faculty of Philosophy at Jena, presented Marx's thesis to the faculty for consideration, Dr. Bachmann noted Marx's intellectual abilities: "The dissertation shows as much spirit and incisiveness as scholarship, wherefore I consider the candidate to be especially deserving."[44] The committee must have thought so too because on April 15, 1841, the University of Jena conferred on Marx the degree of Doctor of Philosophy.

Now qualified to become a university professor, Marx traveled back to the Rhineland in the summer of 1841 to see if he could acquire any more funds from his inheritance—he could not as his university expenses had already exceeded the amount he was supposed to receive— to spend time with his fiancée Jenny, and to join Bruno Bauer as a faculty member at the University of Bonn. Bauer and Marx had also planned to create *Archives of Atheism*, a philosophical journal in which each man would serve as co-editor, but the project did not get off the ground despite contact with potential publishers. When Bauer's atheist and radical beliefs forced him to leave Bonn (even though he had been given options to stay, Bauer did not accept them), Marx had to find another occupation, especially if he wanted to marry Jenny. At this point, their relationship had mostly consisted of letters for the past five years.

---

44. Kamenka, 1983.

In the 1800s, most young men who received doctorate degrees would become professors supported by government funding. As a Young Hegelian with radical beliefs, not only about God but also about the state, Marx had no desire to work for the conservative Prussian government as an academic. Additionally, he had very few in-roads at the universities with his unconventional beliefs and his best shot— a position at Bonn—had just disappeared. Thus, Marx chose a second option that many other Young Hegelians unable to acquire positions at universities selected: journalism.

Marx: The Journalist

Already gaining a reputation for radicalism, Marx was asked to write for a recently founded newspaper called the *Rheinische Zeitung* (*Rhineland News*), a liberal newspaper created in response to the larger *Cologne News*. Dr. Sperber notes that Marx's encounter with the *Rhineland News* played an important role in his life—the newspaper introduced him to communist ideas.[45]

The first issue of the *Rhineland News* came out on January 1, 1842. Robert Jung, a supporter of the Young Hegelians, and Moses Hess, a communist who criticized the atheistic attitudes of the Young Hegelians, spearheaded the proposal, finding as many investors as they could. The paper had three major audiences: Young Hegelians, Prussian authorities, and influential inhabitants of Cologne.

One newspaper, *Cologne News*, dominated the conversation in Cologne and was seen as the mouthpiece of the Cologne elites and insiders. The three audiences mentioned above thought that a newspaper like the *Rhineland News* could stir up the pot some. The Young Hegelians were excited

---

45. Sperber, 2013.

about the possibility of a paper that was more liberal and less Catholic leaning. The Prussian authorities looked forward to a paper that was less anti-Prussian. Finally, influential individuals residing in Cologne (like the Prussian district governor who initially invested in the project) liked the prospect of an additional perspective.

The second editor of the *Rhineland News* was Adolf Rutenberg, a Young Hegelian who was Bruno Bauer's brother-in-law. Because of his connection to Bauer, Marx was given the opportunity to write two long essays for the paper, which appeared in 1842.[46] The first discussed freedom of the press and emphasized its importance in a democracy, particularly in contrast to the very authoritarian Prussian state. The second essay dealt with the atheism of the Young Hegelians, which concerned individuals like Moses Hess who were sympathetic to the communist beliefs of the Young Hegelians, but not the atheism. Marx instead focused on the commonalities of the Young Hegelians and those like Hess: opposition to the authoritarian and Protestant Prussia, which the Catholics of the Rhineland could support.

In late spring 1842, the Prussian government declared that Rutenberg could no longer serve as the editor-in-chief of the *Rhineland News* due to his heavy drinking and refusing to follow the guidelines for Prussian censorship. Rutenberg thus began to work informally while Marx assumed a greater role in editing the paper, beginning in July 1842 and hired officially on October 15, 1842, although he was not the official editor-in-chief—that was the publisher Renard—and did not replace Rutenberg.[47]

---

46. Sperber, 2013.
47. Sperber, 2013.

The Rhineland News, *a newspaper that Marx worked for.*

Adolf Rutenberg was Marx's best friend from the Doctor's Club in Stralau, but Marx and Rutenberg had a falling out after Marx's influence over the *Rhineland News* grew. Marx suggested that he had replaced Rutenberg due to alcoholic excesses, noting to Arnold Ruge that Rutenberg was "absolutely incapable."[48] While circulation and subscriptions were rising, they were not at the level needed even to break even. Marx thus presented himself as a competent successor to the supposedly inept, alcoholic Rutenberg. Dr. Jonathan Sperber believes that Marx may have exaggerated the situation a little bit, given that he replaced Rutenberg as an editor. Even so, Marx's claims did have some validity: Rutenberg held the reputation of being a heavy drinker and supposedly lost a position as a geography teacher at the Royal Prussian Military Academy because of his drinking.[49]

Over six years after Jenny Westphalen's father had indicated to Marx that he wanted the younger man to have a job before he married Jenny, Marx finally had his employment contract that would allow him to marry Jenny. With his contract in hand, Marx moved to Cologne to assume his new role as a leading editor and soon he would bring his bride-to-be to join him.

---

48. Hosfeld, 2012.
49. Sperber, 2013.

CHAPTER 3
Cologne 1842-1843

❧ *"He Will Draw the Eyes of All of Germany Upon Himself"* ❧

Marx: The Editor

 Pierre-Joseph Proudhon—known as the father of anarchism — although he called himself a federalist — actually met Marx when he lived in Paris. The two became friends until Marx wrote a sardonic (grimly cynical) response to Proudhon's *The Philosophy of Poverty*, which Marx ironically titled *The Poverty of Philosophy*. Proudhon's philosophy would spread throughout the world, including in Spain where anarchists would briefly control the city of Barcelona during the Spanish Civil War of 1936-1939.

When Marx moved to Cologne to edit for the *Rhineland News*, he also joined a discussion group about communism, French socialism, and other topics run by Moses Hess. Although the texts that the group read are unknown, contemporary French socialists like Pierre Leroux and Pierre-Joseph Proudhon, the first person to label himself an anarchist according to another anarchist Mikhail Bakunin, may have been read.[50]

---

50. Sperber, 2013.

Pierre-Joseph Proudhon, a father of anarchism.

Moses Hess, although he did not support the atheism of the Young Hegelians, thought extremely highly of Marx. In an 1841 letter to his friend Berthold Auerbach, Hess had the following to say about Marx: "You can prepare yourself to meet the greatest, perhaps the only real, philosopher now living. Soon, when he makes his public *debut* (both as a writer and as an academic), he will draw the eyes of all of Germany upon himself."[51] In addition to noting the influence Hess expected Marx to have in Germany, he went on to explain how Marx is the synthesis, or combination, of a number of well-known philosophers both to those living in the 1800s and some that we could still identify today. Hess even went as far as calling Marx an idol:

> "Dr. Marx — that is the name of my idol — is still a very young man (about 24 years old at most) [Marx was actually 23 at the time] ... Imag-

---

51. Kamenka, 1983.

ine [Jean-Jacques] Rosseau, Voltaire, [Baron] Holbach, [Gotthold Ephraim] Lessing, [Heinrich] Heine and [Georg Wilhelm Friedrich] Hegel all united in one person, I say *united*, not thrown together — and you have Dr. Marx."[52]

Given that these philosophers, especially Rosseau, Voltaire, and Hegel were extremely well regarded in the 1800s, Hess bestowed a high compliment on Marx.

Moses Hess, a Jewish French philosopher.

---

52. Kamenka, 1983.

In mid-October 1842, after Marx became editor of the *Rhineland News*, he composed two pieces, which were included in the paper. The first dealt with the poverty of workers who lived in large apartment houses in Berlin. Marx believed that abolishing private property would improve the situation of these workers. In the second essay, Marx composed a response to a speaker at a Strasbourg conference who talked about the middle class. Marx's argument consisted of three prongs, including an unexpected third proof in which he eschewed (avoided) employing communist ideas. Marx even suggested that any attempts to enact communist ideals should be crushed by the army![53]

Six years before Marx would pen *The Communist Manifesto* with his friend Friedrich Engels, Marx thought that implementation of communist ideals would result in "genuine danger!"[54]

While the *Rhineland News* under Marx was not extremely communist, the Prussian authorities considered the paper radical and demanded an end to the paper. Aware that he would need to look for new employment, Marx quit working for the paper in March 1843, and the *Rhineland News* ceased publication in mid-April 1843, per the Prussian order of January 21, 1843.[55]

The Rhineland was the most independent, industrialized, and socially advanced of the German states, regions, kingdoms, and duchies. Perhaps largely due to the fact that the Rhineland had been a part of revolutionary France between 1795 and 1815 before Prussia annexed it, the elites of Rhenish society were more radical than the rest of Protestant and absolutist Prussia.[56] As a result, many Rhenish people like Marx supported more freedom of the press than those in other regions of the still disunited Germany (unification would not occur until 1871).

53. Sperber, 2013.
54. Sperber, 2013.
55. Sperber, 2013.
56. Thomas, 2013.

Knowing that he would need a new job, Marx inquired about other potential newspaper positions. Arnold Ruge, who helped found the *Rhineland News*, wanted to establish a new paper that would encourage a collaboration of German and French radicals and aptly named the paper, the *Franco-German Yearbooks (Deutsch–Französische Jahrbücher)*. Ruge solicited Marx as a co-editor and promised a salary of 550 talers a year, plus extra for articles that Marx wrote.[57] Marx wanted the paper to originate in Strasbourg, part of France at that time although it was only 2.5 miles west of the Rhine River on the Franco-German border, but Ruge believed Paris would be a better option.

Strasbourg, a part of France.

----

57. Sperber, 2013.

 One of the reasons Marx and Ruge wanted to bring the radicals of Germany and France together is because they observed the common heritage of the French Revolution of 1789. For Marx and others, the French Revolution was the first real revolution. As Dr. McLellan noted, "The Rhineland – where he was born and spent his early life – had been French until 1814, and had enjoyed the benefits of the French Revolution where civil emancipation was a genuine experience and not a possession of foreigners only, to be envied from afar. To all German intellectuals the French Revolution was *the* revolution, and Marx and his Young Hegelian friends constantly compared themselves to the heroes of 1789. Later, Marx would suggest in *The Communist Manifesto* that the French Revolution had paved the way for the upcoming communist revolution (which, by the way, he expected to originate in Germany, not Russia as it actually did) because it abolished feudal property in favor of bourgeois property. Marx also later referred to the 1789 French Revolution as the "great revolution" in *The Communist Manifesto*. In fact, Marx had considered writing a book on the French Revolution. Dr. François Furet, a specialist in the French Revolution, notes, "Marx never did write a book on the French Revolution, although from the beginning to the end of his life and works he devoted numerous comments and allusions to this colossal event."[58]

As Ruge and Marx negotiated the terms of the paper, Marx noted in a March 1843 letter that he intended to get married at the spa town of Kreuznach once he finalized a contract with Ruge. In mid-June 1843 as Jenny and Karl planned to marry in a week, they signed a marriage contract with three separate clauses. The first was biased in the Napoleonic Code and established the communal marital property. The second and third clauses were both to Jenny's advantage: any inheritance became communal property, but debts incurred before marriage did not. Given that Karl could expect some inheritance and Jenny could not, she benefitted. Additionally, Karl had acquired a fair sum of debts, but with the contract, Jenny was not liable for pre-martial debts.

---

58. Furet, 1988.

Marx's Personal and Scholarly Life

On June 19, 1843, Karl Marx married Jenny Westphalen. They had two ceremonies: a civil ceremony — required by the Napoleonic Code — and a religious ceremony at a Protestant church in Kreuznach. They briefly honeymooned on the Rhine River for two weeks and then returned to Kreuznach where Marx spent much time in the library studying prominent political theory works, such as those by Niccolò Machiavelli, Jean-Jacques Rosseau, and Montesquieu. Even so, Marx still had time to spend with Jenny and his new family, namely Jenny's mother and her brother Edgar. Jenny would also become pregnant during this time by early August 1843 although the baby would not be born until Karl and Jenny moved to Paris in 1844.

 Montesquieu's *Spirit of the Laws* (1748) influenced the American founders. In the index to the *Federalist Papers* (documents from the American founders that discuss why our system of government should be adopted), there are 70 references to the classics (for example, Greek and Roman works by Cicero, Livy, Tacitus, Plato, and Aristotle), but only one to the Declaration of Independence. Montesquieu, although not rivaling all the ancient authors, has several references. Even so, Montesquieu differed from the founders. He favored monarchy because an unelected monarch did not have anyone to appease and his power could not be taken away from him.

In addition to spending time reading scholarly material, which he relished, Marx also began a habit that would continue throughout his life: starting works, but not completing them. Marx's critique of Hegel's *Philosophy of Law* was published in the *Franco-German Yearbooks* and planned to expand this critique of Hegel into a larger work, but he never completed it. Similar to what Marx had written about in his essays for the *Rhineland News*, his critique of Hegel's *Philosophy of Law*, entitled the *Critique of Hegel's Philosophy of Right*, showed the influences of Hegel and Feuerbach and focused on comparable political issues. Although Marx had an interesting, albeit brief, passage about democracy, which he would develop in later works, most of the essay was eloquent reiteration of his opinions while serving as the *Rhineland News* editor.

In the *Critique of Hegel's Philosophy of Right*, Marx argued that a good society was a true democracy. The work illustrates Marx's early attempts to criticize current political institutions and argued against Hegel's political philosophy. Hegel had expressed some opinions about the importance of a mediator who spoke on behalf of the people like a monarch, which Marx disliked and argued against. Not surprisingly given Marx's later beliefs, Marx wanted all people to be involved in government and did not like a bureaucracy. While this essay would appear in the *Franco-German Yearbooks*, the newspaper later turned out to be a flop.

 The failure of the *Franco-German Yearbooks* disappointed Marx. He believed that German collaboration with the French would help reduce German backwardness. Marx wanted the Germans to go beyond the French Revolution — the French Revolution was only partial; a German revolution would complete it.[59]

Although Marx would only live in Cologne for six months in 1842-1843 when he served as an editor for the *Rhineland News*, the city of Cologne continued to be a foundation for him where he acquired supporters for the following 10 years. Marx would live in a variety of places abroad, trying to avoid contact with the authorities, which increasingly viewed Marx as radical and unfit to live in many areas in the German Confederation. In fact, Marx did not live in Prussia or even in one of the German Confederation states, choosing instead the more radical Paris, Brussels, and later London. As a result, Marx eventually lost his Prussian citizenship, unable to return to the country in which he was born.

---

59. Furet, 1988.

CHAPTER 4

Paris 1843-1845

⊰ *"A Free Enjoyment of Life"* ⊱

Settling Into Parisian Life

In mid-October of 1843, Karl and Jenny moved to Paris so that Marx could begin work as an editor for the *Franco-German Yearbooks*. Unfortunately, Ruge and Marx had a hard time getting it off the ground, especially with a Prussian government bound and determined to stamp out radicalism. Ruge and Marx had already decided that no Young Hegelians would contribute, except Bruno Bauer, who actually ended up not sending any articles.[60] Although the newspaper was supposed to bring French and German radicals together, the French were not interested. They thought Ruge and Marx did not know much about communism, and they disliked that Ruge and Marx were atheists.[61] While Ruge and Marx were able to interest Germans, a lack of Frenchmen made it practically impossible to live up to the goals of the paper. The paper failed due to money issues and confiscation of issues by the Prussian government. Only one double-issue was published in February 1844, which featured two articles Marx had written.

---

60. McLellan, 2006.
61. McLellan, 2006.

 When Karl and Jenny first moved to Paris, they lived in a communal house. It was originally created by Ruge and based on Fourierist principles (Fourier was a French philosopher and early socialist who advocated for intentional communities, known later as utopian communities).[62] In additional to Karl and Jenny, Ruge proposed that it could house Ruge and his wife, the Herweghs, and the Maurers. Each family would have its own bedroom, but all the families would share the kitchen and the dining room. Additionally, all the wives would take turns cooking dinner. Mrs. Herwegh refused before even moving in. The Marxes lasted for two weeks.

As the Marxes settled into Parisian life, Marx developed an essay entitled "On the Jewish Question." The proper place of Jews in society was a popular topic of philosophers because the Prussian government had given Jews fewer rights than Christians Responding to Bruno Bauer's critique of the Christian state, Marx argued that Bauer did not go far enough and should have criticized the state itself. A hasty reading of the second section of Marx's essay can lead one to believe that he was anti-Semitic since he used the stereotype of Jews as moneylenders and intently focused on making a quick buck. At the same time, Marx also condemns Christianity, arguing instead for a society in which man will not be alienated. But there will be more on this later in Chapter 9.

Despite the failure of the newspaper, Marx stayed in Paris for another three years, pleased with the intellectual culture of the city. His friendship with Ruge, however, did not last. The first tension came when Ruge did not pay Marx for his work with the *Franco-German Yearbooks*, likely due to the fact that the newspaper did not make any money. When Marx noted that he had written two articles, Ruge sent him a complementary issue — not exactly what Marx had in mind.[63] However, the greater break occurred because of Marx's changing beliefs. While Marx did not use the term "communism" in

---

62. McLellan, 2006.
63. McLellan, 2006.

the *Franco-German Yearbooks*, he labeled himself a communist by the spring of 1844. Ruge, on the other hand, strongly disagreed with communism. When the two men disagreed publicly in published articles about the weaver's revolt in the Prussian region of Silesia in the summer of 1844, the damage was irreparable. The friendship could not withstand these differences in political opinion and thus ended. Marx also ended his friendship with Herwegh, although he would remain close to Heine.

 In early June 1844, Silesian (a region in Central Europe, mostly located in Poland) weavers revolted against the factory owners' luxurious and extravagant lifestyles. In the villages of Peterswaldau and Langenbielau, the weavers protested low wages by destroying the houses and property of the factory owners. When troops were sent in to suppress the revolt, 11 individuals were killed, and 200 weavers and three soldiers were wounded. Many, including Karl Marx, point to this event as the beginning of the German labor movement.

As Marx's friendship with Ruge cooled, Jenny gave birth to a girl, named Jenny after her mother, on May 1, 1844. Baby Jenny was a sickly infant, so Jenny took the baby back to Trier from May to September. Jenny wanted to see her family, specifically her mother, and ask her old doctor about how to help the baby. During her time in Trier, Jenny tentatively reached out to her mother-in-law, who originally had not been very supportive of her relationship with Karl, and found that Marx's mother was actually quite nice. Jenny also acquired a wet nurse. Even so, Jenny found some aspects of the otherwise pleasant trip disagreeable, namely all the friends and relatives who wanted to hold the baby. As Dr. McLellan noted, "When her old friends and acquaintances came to see her and hold the baby, she felt as if she were holding court."[64] Nonetheless, Jenny stayed in Trier for four months, but near the end of her stay, expressed urgent desire to be back in Paris with Marx to make sure her husband was on the straight and narrow.

---

64. McLellan, 2006.

Marx, however, was likely too focused on his writing to be tempted by the city. With his wife and baby daughter home with family, Marx had plenty of time to write. He made copious notes on economics, communism, and Hegel. Although these works, known as the Economic and Philosophical Manuscripts, the Paris Manuscripts, or the 1844 Manuscripts, were published posthumously in 1932, they were the foundations of Marx's understanding of economics. In fact, the 1844 Manuscripts later influenced Marx's four-part tome, *Das Kapital.*

The manuscripts can be divided into three sections — wages, capital, and rent — and clearly demonstrate Hegel's influence on Marx. Marx believed that a man ought to control himself: with religion, man gives control to God; with economics, man gives control to money. After describing four different ways man can be alienated, Marx ends with a description of a future communist society, noting that "[m]y work would be a free expression of my life and therefore a free enjoyment of my life."[65]

Friedrich Engels, inextricably connected to Marx, believed that one can see the three major elements of Marx's thought although they were not yet united, namely German idealism, French socialism, and English economics.

While Marx would later expound upon the thoughts and statements in these manuscripts and give greater detail, these 1844 manuscripts were a starting point for him. His vision after 1844 did not change: Germany must bring about a revolution that leads to a communist society. Interestingly, just as Marx was beginning to articulate his communist beliefs, he became friends with Engels, who would be by his side for the rest of Marx's life.

---

65. McLellan, 2006.

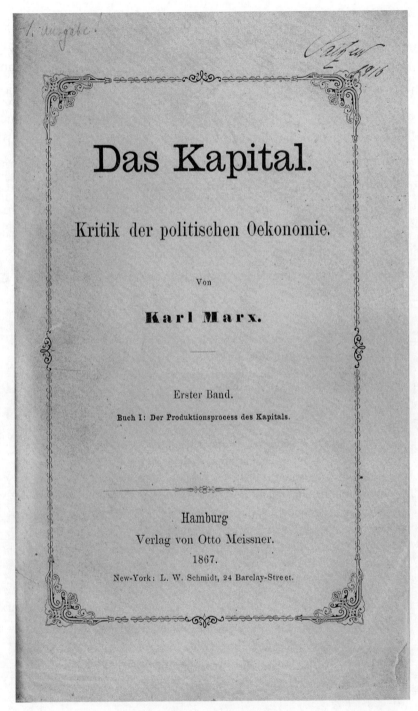

Das Kapital, one of Marx's works.

Marx and Engels

Marx and Engels actually met while Marx was an editor for the *Rhineland News*. But Marx did not like Engels because of his connection with a paper that he disliked: the *Freien*. Marx, however, reconsidered his thoughts when he read some of Engels's work. Marx had first become acquainted with Engels's beliefs when he read Engels's essay in the one issue of the *Franco-German Yearbooks* entitled "Outline of a Critique of Political Economy." Marx had been so impressed with the essay that he included excerpts in his 1844 manuscripts. The two men had corresponded, and they met again on August 28, 1844 at the Café de la Régence on the Place du Palais, a famous café that had served Voltaire, Benjamin Franklin, and Louis Napoleon among others. Engels left a much more favorable impression on Marx and so began a lifelong friendship.

 You probably know that Marx wrote *The Communist Manifesto* with Friedrich Engels in 1848, but you may not know much about Engels. He was German socialist philosopher born in the Rhine on November 28, 1820. Around the time that he began working as an office clerk at a commercial house in Bremen in 1838, Engels became acquainted with the works of Hegel. In 1841, Engels briefly joined the Prussian Army as a member of the Household Artillery. After Engels started to express radical ideas, his father sent him to work for the textile firm of Ermen and Engels. The plan was not successful. In fact, Engels's experiences and his personal observations of the horrendous working conditions of the British workers inspired him to write *The Conditions of the Working Class in England in 1844*. While in Manchester, Engels met Mary Burns, the woman with whom he would be in relationship until her death in 1862. Acting as his guide in Manchester, Burns introduced Engels to the British working class. Although they were together throughout their lives, Engels and Burns never married because Engels believed that marriage was unnatural and unjust.

After Marx's death in 1883, Engels was the established authority on Marx and Marxism and would help edit the second and third volume of *Das Kapital*. Although Vladimir Ilyich Lenin, who helped initiate the Communist Revolution in Russia in 1917, regarded Marx as the pinnacle of the proletariat, Lenin considered Engels a close second:

"After his friend Karl Marx (who died in 1883), Engels was the finest scholar and teacher of the modern proletariat in the whole civilised world. From the time that fate brought Karl Marx and Frederick Engels together, the two friends devoted their life's work to a common cause. And so to understand what Frederick Engels has done for the proletariat, one must have a clear idea of the significance of Marx's teaching and work for the development of the contemporary working-class movement."[66]

Interestingly, Lenin composed this panegyric (a public text in praise of someone) over 20 years before the Communist Revolution in Russia.

Marx and Engels had hit it off so well when they met for the second time that they decided to spend the next 10 days together in the rue Vaneau. There, they planned to write a 30-page pamphlet, which responded to Bruno Bauer, with whom Marx now found himself disagreeing. The pamphlet turned into a 300-page book that was published in February 1845 and entitled *The Holy Family*, an ironic reference to the Bauer brothers.

In the book, subtitled "Critique of Critical Criticism," Marx developed his materialist conception of history (meaning that Marx focused on physical things rather than mentioning a higher being), praised the anarchist Proudhon for being the first thinker to question private property and questioned Bauer's view of the French Revolution. Bauer believed the masses had contaminated the ideas of the French Revolution. Marx, by contrast, thought the masses of the French Revolution were only a starting point and should go further. Although not one of Marx's major works, *The Holy Family* demonstrates Marx's developing thoughts, his break with previous influences, and his growing friendship with Engels.

---

66. Lenin, 1896.

Vorwärts!, a radical biweekly newspaper.

Before *The Holy Family* could be published, the French Minister of the Interior Guizot required Marx and other radicals who had assisted with *Vorwärts!* (Forward! or Advance!) to leave Paris. *Vorwärts!* was a radical bi-weekly newspaper that had contributions from Heine, Herwegh, Bakunin, Ruge, Engels, and of course, Marx (among others). American feminist and transcendentalist Margaret Fuller even translated a piece by Heinrich Börnstein, the publisher of this most radical newspaper in Europe, in an attempt to bring some of the radicalism in Europe to America.[67] French King Louis Philippe reportedly said, "We must purge Paris of German philosophers!" Informed on January 25, 1845, Marx was supposed to leave within a day given the perimeters of the grace period. Forever the rebel, Marx left on February 2 with no consequences to a city that welcomed radicals: Brussels.

Marx abandoned his Prussian nationality in December 1845. He thought about immigrating to the United States and even applied to the major of Trier for a permit, but reconsidered and decided instead to forsake his nationality. Thus, from 1846 to the end of his life in 1883, Marx was stateless and did not have a nationality.

67. Capper and Giorcelli, 2008.

CHAPTER 5
Brussels 1845-1848

⊰} *"The Point is to Change It"* {⊱

Marx's Growing Family and Growing Number of Projects

Brussels was an ideal location for Marx because it was in the middle of a triangle of radicalism: London was to the northwest, Paris to the southwest, and Cologne to the southeast. Because Belgium enjoyed greater freedom of expression, political refugees and radicals came from all of Europe. Brussels was Marx's home for three years — likely the happiest time of Marx's life, since he had a comfortable income and time to pursue intellectual interests.[68]

It was at this time, April 1845, that Jenny's mother sent her daughter a maid, Helene Demuth, to assist with the household. This was especially helpful, given that Jenny had recently discovered that she was pregnant again. Helene would remain with the family for the duration of Marx's life and later ran Engels's household for seven years after Marx died until her death in 1890. Known by the nicknames of Lenchen or Nim, Helene Demuth had such a close connection with the Marx family that she was buried in the Marx family grave in accordance with Jenny Marx's wishes.

---

68. McLellan, 2006.

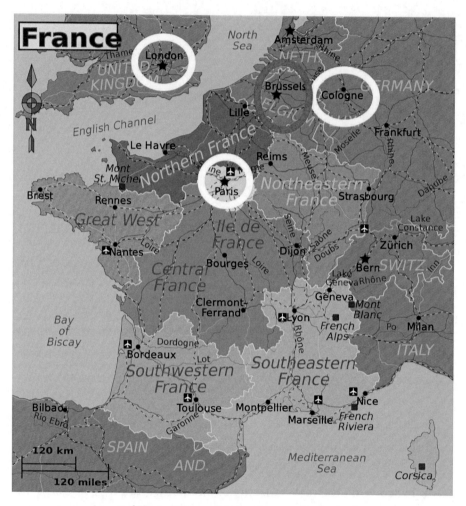

A map of Western Europe showing the triangle of radicalism.

Helene Demuth, the maid of Jenny, Marx's wife.

In line with his past and future habits, Marx began three projects that he did not complete and spent a large amount of time studying in libraries, first in Brussels and later in London with Engels. The first project, *A Critique of Economics and Politics* was intended to expand upon his themes in *Critique of Hegel's Philosophy of Right* and *The Jewish Question*, Marx even signed a contract, and Engels announced in a newspaper that the book was in print.[69] But it was not to be. Marx only finished the table of contents of the political half.

Engels, who was currently in Barmen finishing *Conditions of the Working Class in England*, kept sending publishing projects to Marx. He agreed to collaborate on two of the suggestions: the first dealt with protective tariffs,

---

69. McLellan, 2006.

the second with utopian socialists.[70] Like Marx's *A Critique of Economics and Politics*, neither of these projects came to be. Instead, Marx immersed himself in the municipal library in Brussels, reading French works on economics.

The German Ideology *based on the philosophy of Ludwig Feuerbach.*

---

70. McLellan, 2006.

Marx did have time to compose his now famous 11 theses on Feuerbach, which formed the basis of a book detailing Marx's new philosophy history entitled *The German Ideology*. The most famous thesis is the last: "Philosophers have hitherto only interpreted the world in various ways; the point is to change it." Marx wanted to keep German criticism, but move it into practical material and political terms. The 11th thesis would be used by many communists later and is engraved in the entryway of Humboldt University in Berlin. Perhaps most significantly, it is engraved on Marx's tombstone in Highgate Cemetery in London in addition to the last line of *The Communist Manifesto*: "Workers of the world, unite!"

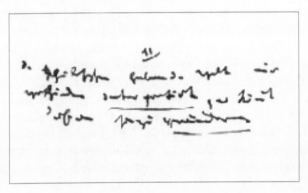

"Philosophers have hitherto only interpreted the world in various ways; the point is to change it." – The 11th thesis of The German Ideology.

While Marx only had one short work to show for his first couple months in Brussels, it is clear that he was tossing ideas around in his head. In the preface to the 1888 English Edition of *The Communist Manifesto*, Engels noted that Marx and he intended to do for history what Charles Darwin had done for biology. Marx definitely supported this opinion — he wrote a letter to Engels and told him to link Marx's work to Darwin. Marx knew, of course, that Darwin and he approached history differently. Darwin was backward looking while Marx was forward looking. According to Marx, growth and history have the same pattern, thus pointing to the need for revolution. In fact, Marx even suggests that everything before the Revolution was merely the pre-history of humanity. Both men worked independently, and when Engels met Marx in Brussels in the spring of 1845, "he had it already worked out and put it before me in terms almost as clear as those in which I have stated it here."[71]

 Each age has its great men. Some are political or military leaders like Alexander the Great and Julius Caesar. More recently, though, theologians and philosophers have led the way. For example, Martin Luther and John Calvin inspired the Reformation while John Locke, Gottfried Wilhelm Leibniz (he invented calculus!), Voltaire, and Jean-Jacques Rousseau stimulated the Enlightenment. The men who probably most influenced the modern world were none other than Charles Darwin and Karl Marx. As you probably know, Darwin founded a new branch of life science known as evolutionary biology. What you might not know is that Darwin replaced Aristotle's Chain of Being, a concept stating that life is ultimately tending toward greater perfection that had been universally accepted by scientists, with the idea that purely material processes can explain the living world.[72] Even so, Darwin was not a strict atheist: "When thus reflecting I feel compelled to look at a First Cause having an intelligent mind in some degree analogous to that of man; and I deserve to be called a theist."[73] He suggests in the *Origin of Species* that God uses natural selection. God has not imposed his divine will, but rather established general laws. Thus, an individual does not need to question the reasoning and rationales of God; it simply is better in nature. This belief allows for a buffer between evil and God.

In July 1845, Karl and Jenny occupied themselves with two different activities: Karl went to England with Engels while Jenny journeyed back to Trier to be with her lonely mother. Marx and Engels spent most of their time reading in the Old Chetham Library in Manchester, England.[74] A very pregnant Jenny had originally planned a shorter visit, but ended up staying for two months so that she could spend more time with her mother.

---

71. Engels, 1969.
72. Mayr, 2009.
73. Corey, 1994.
74. McLellan, 2006.

As a result, Karl and Jenny's second daughter named Laura Marx was born in Trier, rather than in London, on September 26, 1845.

With Jenny away, Marx and Engels jointly began to work in late September 1845 on expanding Marx's 11 theses on Feuerbach into a full-sized book, which he entitled *The German Ideology*. Unsurprisingly given his habit of starting, but not completing works, Marx finished only about 100 pages before he abandoned the project a year later in August 1846. Ironically, although the book was supposed to focus on critiques of Feuerbach with additional criticisms against Bruno Bauer and Max Stirner, the section on Feuerbach was largely unfinished. Since Marx had already dedicated a book to critiquing Bauer's opinions, namely *The Holy Family*, the section on Bauer was quite short. By contrast, while the section on Feuerbach was the most important for Marx's later philosophy, the section on Stirner was the longest, lengthier than the other parts combined.[75]

Most of the section on Stirner, who Marx and Engels call "Saint Max," is simply a harsh appraisal of Stirner's beliefs, although there are sections of interest, especially several which sound similar to passages in *The Communist Manifesto*. For example, to respond to Stirner who suggested that everyone would have to do everything in a communist society with division of labor, Marx and Engels observed, "[E]ach should do the work of Raphael, but that anyone in whom there is a potential Raphael should be able to develop without hindrance."[76] Marx did not like specialization. He wanted to give everyone the opportunity to try a variety of activities. Similarly, Marx and Engels noted, "In a communist society there are no painters but, at most, people who engage in painting among other activities."[77] Marx and Engels did not want people to be tied to a specific job, but instead have the

---

75. McLellan, 2006.
76. McLellan, 2006.
77. McLellan, 2006.

opportunity to try a lot of different jobs. In *The Communist Manifesto*, the language is almost identical: "In place of the old bourgeois society with its classes and class antagonisms we shall have an association, in which the free development of each is the condition for the free development of all."[78]

A page from The German Ideology.

---

78. Marx and Engels, 2011.

In other words, Marx and Engels believed that a man should not be enslaved to a particular job. He should have the opportunity to be whatever he wants to be whenever he wants it. In contrast to older traditions that emphasized the value of work (and rest!), Marx did not leave any shred of the dignity of work. He wanted to liberate man from work. Thus, Stirner completely misunderstood Marx's position when the former argued that everyone had to do everything. Rather, Marx posited that anyone could do anything.

The most significant passage, however, gave an example of communism. Marx and Engels's example of communism was set in a rural society. They famously mentioned three activities that would occur after the Communist Revolution, noting that in current society, a man must choose to be a hunter, a fisherman, a herdsman, or a critical critic to maintain his livelihood. By contrast,

> "in communist society, where nobody has one exclusive sphere of activity but each can become accomplished in any branch he wishes, society regulates the general production and thus makes it possible for me to do one thing today and another tomorrow, to hunt in the morning, fish in the afternoon, rear cattle in the evening, criticize [sic] after dinner, just as I have a mind, without ever becoming hunter, fisherman, herdsman, or critic."[79]

Thus, communist society was more beneficial to the individual as he or she did not have to be trapped in one job, but could do anything at any time.

The second volume discussed what Marx and Engels called "true socialism," also known as German utopian socialism. Although well known today, *The German Ideology* was unknown for almost a century. Despite

---

79. Marx and Engels, 1972.

Marx and Engels's attempts to find a publisher, only a short section was published.

Marx's Political Activities

Now having laid out his philosophical positions and his communist views, Marx next moved to political activities. Along with Engels and others, Marx tried to establish a Communist Correspondence Committee, which was the origin of the later Communist Internationals. It was Marx's first foray (attempt to become involved in a new activity or sphere) into practical politics, and he struggled somewhat with winning friends and influencing people. In addition to disagreeing with revolutionary Weitling, Marx also quarreled with Proudhon, who was to be a Paris correspondent for the committee.

 Dr. Menger noted that some of the denunciations of Proudhon might not have originated with Marx. In fact, "Marx had attacked Proudhon in a pamphlet [*The Poverty of Philosophy*] full of quotations from Thompson, to one of which Thompson's name was attached." In other words, Marx used Thompson's words to attack Proudhon, but only cited Thompson once; Marx didn't always cite his sources, which you should do![80]

In response to a letter from Proudhon listing several reservations about the committee, Marx produced in late 1846 and early 1847 a two-volume book entitled *The Poverty of Philosophy*, a spin-off of the title of one of Proudhon's recent books, *The Philosophy of Poverty*. In his work, Marx mainly complained that Proudhon did not understand the historical development of man and instead presented the first delineation of the materialist view of history. The book was both extremely popular when it came out and later. In fact, Marx considered *The Poverty of Philosophy* to be an introduction for his later work, *Das Kapital*. Interestingly, Proudhon had an

---

80. Chapman, 1899.

annotated copy of Marx's book, perhaps planning to respond before the 1848 revolutions broke out.[81]

As Marx was developing some of his most important ideas, he also expressed a significant change in his personal life. On February 3, 1847, Karl and Jenny welcomed another child into the world: their first boy, Edgar Marx. Karl adored his son, named after Jenny's brother Edgar, and referred to his boy as "Musch," or little fly. Tragically, the boy would die on April 6, 1855 at the age of eight after a month-long illness, probably from a ruptured appendix or tuberculosis.

Around the time that Marx, Engels, and others worked to establish a correspondence committee: the London Central Committee. In November 1846, the committee changed its name and became the League. The First Congress of the League assembled in London from June 2-9, 1847 and decided to work on four items:

1. Reorganization of the democratic basis of the League

2. Issuance of a periodical

3. Change of name from simply the League to the Communist League

4. Emphasis of the necessity of avoiding conspiratorial tendencies

The newly founded Communist League had a three-tiered structure: commune, circle committee (which included the chairman and treasurers of relevant communes), and central committee. Two events of the congress had special significance. First, the new statutes replaced the previous slogan — "All Men are Brothers" — with a slogan similar to Marx's now famous line — "Proletarians of all Countries – Unite!" Second, and much more importantly, Engels was to draft a "Confession of Faith" — a statement of

81. McLellan, 2006.

one's principles — for the Second Congress in November 1847. This was the beginning of *The Communist Manifesto*.

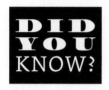 Marx reportedly is the reason why the slogan of the Communist League was changed. Supposedly, Marx stated that he did not want to be a brother to many men.[82]

At the Second Congress from November 29 to December 8, 1847, the attendees decided to reword the somewhat utopian statutes from the First Congress and replace them with four essential aims:

1. Overthrow of the bourgeoisie (the wealthy middle class)

2. Domination of the proletariat (the working class)

3. Abolition of bourgeois society with class antagonisms

4. Establishment of a new society without classes and private property

In light of the new foci, the congress commissioned Marx and Engels to write a manifesto delineating the views of the Communist League. This manifesto, of course, became *The Communist Manifesto*, which was arguably the most important work composed in the 1800s.

 The words "bourgeoisie" and "bourgeois" are very similar, but they have two different functions in a sentence. The bourgeoisie is a French term that originally meant those who lived in the borough, that is, in the city. In Marxist thought, the bourgeoisie refers to the property owning and ruling class of capitalist society. Bourgeois is a singular word, which can either refer to the characteristics of the ruling class or a singular bourgeois person.

---

82. McLellan, 2006.

At first, however, Marx did not feel particularly inclined to write and instead focused on giving a course of lectures about capital (financial assets) to the German Workers' Education Association in January 1848. When Marx and Engels began work on the manifesto, they went through three tentative drafts, two of which were confessions of faith and the third, entitled "Principles of Communism," contained a catechism (normally a summary of Christian doctrine) of 25 questions and answers. Engels suggested dropping the catechism, which Marx did although he relied heavily on this third draft. Even though Engels had originally crafted the catechistic version, Engels later noted that *The Communist Manifesto* was essentially Marx's works. There are four main sections, which we will discuss later in Chapter 9. The manifesto was finished and published in February 1848.

 The Revolutions of 1848 affected almost every country in Europe. Some notable exceptions were England, which was distinct in its political government; Russia, a part of Europe, but very backward; and Spain, which was very Catholic and had established a system of consistent peaceful changes of political parties. The liberal revolutions were against the monarchies all across Europe and mostly occurred in cities with a middle class, university students, and urban working people. The revolutions had three stages, beginning in France, moving to Germany and Italy, and spreading to Prussia and the Austrian Empire. They ultimately failed, as liberal nationalists did not get democratic reform. Former Secretary of State known for his knowledge of foreign affairs Henry Kissinger said that the balance of power finally fell apart because of nationalism, the revolutions of 1848, and the Crimean War of 1854-1856 (all of which Marx wrote about).

Paradoxically, the publication of *The Communist Manifesto* did not attract much interest as the majority of Europe erupted in revolutions, now known as the Revolutions of 1848. While initially successful and ubiquitous throughout Europe, the conservative European monarchs, intent to preserve order, squelched all of the revolutions by 1849. Reacting to the news of the revolution in Paris, the Belgian government decided to crack down on the refugees currently residing in Brussels and included Marx on a list of foreigners to deport because they correctly suspected that Marx had used some of his 6,000-franc inheritance from his mother to finance revolutionary activities.[83] Thus mandated and further goaded by a local police commissioner at 1 in the morning, Karl and Jenny quickly left Brussels for Paris. They would not stay there for long, however, and instead decided to relocate to Cologne.

83. McLellan, 2006.

CHAPTER 6
Cologne II 1848-1849

⇥ *"He is No Journalist and Will Never Become One"* ⇤

Now back in his birth region, the Rhineland, Marx went to work establishing a radical newspaper. The name for this new project, while not creative, harkened back to Marx's time at his first newspaper: the *New Rhineland News (Neue Rheinische Zeitung)*. Marx planned for the paper to focus on more than simply news in Cologne; he wanted it to include information of national interest.

The *New Rhineland News* was supposed to be the successor of the previous Cologne newspaper *Rhineland News*, which Marx edited briefly and which had been suppressed by state censors. Marx, Engels, and some other members of the Communist League founded the paper when Marx and Engels returned to Germany after the outbreak of the 1848 Revolutions. The newspaper criticized the Prussian and Austrian monarchist counter-revolution responses as well as the tendency of the German bourgeoisie to take the side of the monarchists.

Marx was disappointed to discover that he would not find the same revolutionary atmosphere as Paris because the revolutions in Germany had only been prominent in two cities — Berlin and Vienna. Nonetheless, Marx remained focused on highlighting two main points in the *New Rhineland*

News: a single, united German republic and restoration of Poland (which would require a war with Russia).[84] The paper was not strictly a communist or worker's paper. Instead, the subtitle chosen — "An Organ of Democracy" — indicated that Marx wanted to reach a broader audience. Through the paper, Marx sought to encourage workers to assist the bourgeoisie in their revolution.

While the *New Rhineland News* a circulation of 6,000, making it one of the largest left-wing newspapers in Germany, it did not have enough shareholders and had to rely instead on subscriptions.[85] Thus, the newspaper, although recognized by historians as one of the most important daily paper regarding the Revolutions of 1848 in Germany, would have a short press run: June 1, 1848 to May 19, 1849. In its short life, a total of 301 editions were produced, and Marx himself wrote at least 80 articles.[86] This work likely prepared Marx for the countless newspaper articles he (or his ghostwriter, Engels) would compose for the *New York Tribune*. Even so, Stephen Born, an occasional visitor to the newspaper office, noted that Marx was no journalist and never would be: "He pores for a whole day over a leading articles that would take someone else a couple hours as though it concerned the handling of a deep philosophical problem."[87]

Marx's brief success with the *New Rhineland News*, however, did not ingratiate him to the Prussian government. He was arrested and tried on a charge of encouraging armed insurrection (violent uprising against an authority of government). Although Marx was acquitted, he was expelled from Germany (despite his earlier attempts in 1848 to reacquire Prussian citizenship), briefly lived in Paris until he was kicked out, and would live abroad in England for the rest of his life.

---

84. McLellan, 2006.
85. Sperber, 1994.
86. Johnson, Walker, and Gray, 2014.
87. McLellan, 2006.

 In America, *The New York Tribune* under Horace Greeley and *The New York Times* under Henry Jarvis Raymond were the most popular newspapers in the 1840s. The *Tribune* was known for its sympathetic approach to a variety of ideas and beliefs common in the 1840s and 1850s. The *Times*, as Raymond announced in the first issue, intended to discuss controversial topics in as dispassionate language as possible. Raymond believed that men should be guided by reason rather than passion.

CHAPTER 7
London I 1849-1859

⊰ *The Second as Farce* ⊱

London: Marx's Final Home

As mentioned earlier, London was a part of a triangle of revolutionary cities. When the Prussian authorities in Cologne forced Marx and his family
to move elsewhere, they wanted to select another revolutionary city that
would be more welcoming to them. Even so, Marx did not intend to spend
the rest of his life in London. He came only as a temporary resident with
hopes of returning to the continent when more revolutions broke out.
Sadly for Marx, despite his ever-present optimism and expectation, the
revolutionary fervor of 1848 never returned. Thus, London became Marx's
home more by accident than by intention.

Marx arrived in London in August 1849, while Jenny would arrive later in
September. The first order of business was to acquire a house, as Jenny was
extremely pregnant with their fourth child. On November 5, 1849, Karl
and Jenny welcomed another child into the world, Heinrich Guido, known
as Foxchen. The family also called him Little Fawkes in honor of Guy
Fawkes, a conspirator among a group of English Catholics who planned
the failed Gunpowder Plot of November 1805 — an attempt to assassinate

King James I and put a Catholic monarch on the throne.[88] Heinrich's middle name Guido may also be a reference to Guy Fawkes, as the conspirator was also known as Guido Fawkes. Tragically, little Heinrich died from convulsions resulting from meningitis a little over a year later while still an infant. He would be the first of three Marx children to die in London on Dean Street. Marx also found himself moving his family several times because of a lack of cash. Thus, on a personal front, London proved to be a challenging area for Marx, and he again contemplated immigrating to the United States. He would have done so had the ticket not been so expensive.

 All four of Karl and Jenny's oldest children were born in different countries: Jennychen in Paris, France; Laura in Trier, Prussia (now Germany); Edgar in Brussels, Holland; and Heinrich Guido in London, England.

From a political perspective, however, Marx quickly got involved in three activities: assisting refugees through the German Workers' Educational Association, starting a monthly journal similar to the *New Rhineland News*, and reorganizing the Communist League. On the side, Marx also gave lectures about property from the Association of German Refugees from November 1849 to the early part of 1850. Marx also had time for fun, and he participated in fencing and chess with the Association![89]

Split of the Communist League

In 1850, the Communist League split into two factions: the London group and the Cologne group. Marx oversaw the former while August Willich and Karl Schapper lead the latter. Although Marx would regularly try to promote more unity between the two sides, he was spurned by many of the

---

88. McLellan, 2006.
89. McLellan, 2006.

Cologne communists. Marx also became president of the London Central Committee of the Communist League and desired to bring the London and Cologne communists together, as the two groups had often disagreed. To bring about this change, he delivered a now famous address in 1850 in which he stated that workers could come alongside democrats in order to bring about the revolution more quickly.

 Willich and Bartholemy challenged Marx to a duel because they believed he was too conservative. Marx ignored them and did not fight. Conrad Schramm, a young associate of Marx's, "was less prudent" and insulted Willich, forcing a duel. The duel took place on the sea coast of Belgium, and although Schramm was wounded, he survived the encounter.[90]

Despite attempts to reconcile the two parties, the Cologne group and London group grew apart and functioned as independent entities with only loose connections. Marx condemned the minority, or Cologne group, and claimed that they replaced a materialist understanding with an idealist one. They acknowledged the disadvantages of the proletariat while still praising Germany: "Just as the Democrats made a sort of holy entity out of the word people, you are doing the same with the word proletariat."[91] For the next two years until 1852 when the Communist League dissolved, these two factions continued to fight.

Optimistic about the possibility of another revolutionary outbreak in Europe after the Revolutions of 1848, Marx busied himself in 1849 and 1850 with bringing about a new paper: *Neue Rheinische Zeitung-Politisch-Oekonomisch Revue* (*New Rhineland News-Political-Economic Review*). As the title indicated, Marx wanted to connect back to the *New Rhineland News*, which he had hoped would assist with the Revolutions of 1848, and bring together socio-economic ideas with political activity. The *Review*

---

90. Spargo, 1910.
91. Mehring, 2003.

lasted longer than the *Franco-German Yearbooks*, but not by much. Five issues were published in 1850, and Marx and Engels wrote many of the articles, which predominantly discussed the failure of the Revolutions of 1848.

Eighteenth Brumaire of Louis Napoleon

Because the *Review* did not take off, Marx was forced to turn to other writing venues. Ever the man to respond to current events and happenings, Marx composed a well-known pamphlet entitled *The Eighteenth Brumaire of Louis Napoleon*, which was published in 1852. Referring back to Napoleon Bonaparte's coup in 1799, known as 18 Brumaire Year VIII in the Republican Calendar, Marx discussed Louis Napoleon Bonaparte's seizure of power on December 2, 1851 when the latter turned himself from president into Emperor Napoleon III.

In *Brumaire*, Marx developed thoughts he had begun to consider in some articles he had written for the *Review*, which Engels later republished as *The Class Struggles in France*. Both works demonstrate Marx's attempts to discuss events in modern history from a materialist perspective. While Marx still considered France the center of revolutions, he mused that the 1848 revolutions ultimately failed because they tried to make the revolutions a rerun of the 1789 Revolution. Given this background, Marx's first passage of the work (and often cited line) makes much more sense: "Hegel remarks somewhere that all facts and personages of great importance occur, as it were, twice. He forgot to add: the first time as tragedy, the second as farce."[92] Louis Napoleon's coup was only a farce of Napoleon's, meaning that while the 1789 Revolution was somewhat successful, doing the same thing again as in the Revolutions of 1848 would not be.

---

92. Illingworth, 2011.

Likewise, the 1848 Revolutions were a charade, even mockery, of the 1789 revolution. Louis Napoleon was able to step in because none of the other classes — bourgeoisie, petty bourgeoisie, or proletariat — had been able to lead society. With *Brumaire*, Marx was hopeful about an imminent revolution, but the likelihood of a political revolution in Paris was declining. While Marx's hope was unrealized, this work (along with *The Class Struggles in France*) is valuable because it is one of the early examples of historical materialism (remember, this means focusing on physical things, rather than spiritual). In fact, *Brumaire* was one of Marx's most successful works, including people beyond his followers. It was published in New York, but not many copies circulated in Europe.

Brumaire, named after the French word for fog, brume, was the second month in the French Republican Calendar. It was named for the fog occurred frequently then in France. Brumaire was the second month of the autumn quarter and started around October 22 and ended about a month later. The month before Brumaire is Vendémiaire (meaning grape harvester), and the month after is Frimaire (meaning frost).

French Months (used 1793-1805)	Normal Months
Vendémiaire (September 22 to October 21)	September and October
Brumaire (October 22 to November 20)	October and November
Frimaire (November 21 to December 20)	November and December

Die Revolution,

Eine Zeitschrift in zwanglosen Heften.

Herausgegeben von

J. Weydemeyer.

Erstes Heft.

Der 18te Brumaire des Louis Napoleon

von

Karl Marx.

New-York.

Expedition: Deutsche Vereins-Buchhandlung von Schmidt und Helmich.
William-Street Nr. 191.

1852.

The well-known pamphlet, The Eighteenth Brumaire of Louis Napoleon.

The Cologne Communist Trial of 1852

Around the time *Brumaire* was published, the Communist League experienced a setback with the Cologne Communist Trial on October 4, 1852. Kaiser Wilhelm II wanted a show trial to blame the 1848 Revolution in Germany on a conspiracy. Eleven men suspected of being communists were arrested in 1851 and put on trial for high treason in 1852. Per usual, Marx penned a series of articles reflecting on the events that he later turned into a book, *Reflections about the Communist Trial in Cologne*, which could be read freely in America, although it had to be smuggled into several European countries. In the end, seven of the 11 men were found guilty and sentenced for three to six years' imprisonment in a fortress.

Just as Marx oversaw the inner workings of the London group of the Communist League, August Willich and Karl Schapper helped direct the Cologne group. When the 11 men were arrested in 1851 for the Cologne Communist Trial, the League did not exist in Germany in an organized form. Marx tried raise money for their Cologne brothers and submitted reviews to British newspapers to object to their arrest. In addition to his efforts to protest the Cologne Communist arrest and trial, Marx presided over a group of roughly 20 men in London that met regularly in 1851 and 1852. This group was known as "the Synagogue" or "The Marx Society."[93] After the guilty verdict, however, Marx no longer saw the Communist League as "opportune," and recommended that the league dissolve itself, which it did.[94] As a result, Marx would not be involved in politics from 1852 to 1859.

---

93. McLellan, 2006.
94. McLellan, 2006.

DID YOU KNOW? August Willich, the co-leader of the left fraction of the Communist League who took an active part in the Revolutions of 1848, came to the United States in 1853. In 1858, he moved from Brooklyn to Cincinnati to serve as editor of the *German Republican*, a German-language free labor newspaper. He would keep this role until the beginning of the Civil War. Known as one of the "Ohio Hegelians," Willich joined the 9th Ohio Infantry ("Die Neuner"), filled with other German immigrants, with the outbreak of the Civil War in 1861. He later become a major general in the Union Army.

August Willich, the co-leader of the left fraction of the Communist League.

487 Newspaper Articles

Instead, Marx turned to journalism, but in a way that was much more lucrative than his failed attempts to start radical papers. He began writing as a European correspondent for the *New York Daily Tribune*. It was not completely Marx, though, as Engels somewhat regularly ghostwrote articles for Marx. The articles were successful and often reprinted in other papers, such as *The Free Press*, *Das Volk*, *The People's Paper*, and *Die Reform*.

From 1852 to 1863, Marx — and Engels — wrote for six different newspapers that spanned the globe from the United States to the United Kingdom to Prussia and Austria and finally to South Africa. Most of Marx's articles appeared in the *New York Tribune* due to Marx's connection with Charles Anderson Dana. The top aide to Horace Greeley and the managing editor of the Republican newspaper the *New York Tribune*, Dana met Marx in Cologne in November 1848 and offered Marx a job writing a series of articles about the revolutions in Europe. Unbeknownst to Dana, Engels ghostwrote many articles because Marx's English was not good. In any case, Dana liked Marx's articles and requested more articles. After July 1852, Marx started to write in English on his own.[95]

 Horace Greeley was an extremely well-recognized figure in the 1800s. He was the founder and editor of the *New York Tribune*, one of the most popular newspapers of his time, and he helped organize and found the Republican Party in 1854 and assisted in securing the nomination for Abraham Lincoln. He also unsuccessfully ran against incumbent President Ulysses S. Grant as a Liberal Republican in the 1872 presidential election.

---

95. McLellan, 2006.

Marx was paid for 487 articles although Engels wrote most of the military articles.[96] Although Marx is well known for *The Communist Manifesto* and *Das Kapital,* he covered and wrote more of these articles than anything else he published. They were also more lucrative than Marx's other published writings. Although today we do not identify Marx as a journalist, Engels emphasized this aspect of Marx's life in the latter's eulogy. Engels did not mention *The Communist Manifesto* directly, but he did mention all of the newspapers on which Marx worked, including the *New York Tribune.*[97]

He tended to focus on three main topics in his journalism: the Crimean War (1854-1856) and its significance for foreign policy and for Britain; the British Empire in Asia, including the Opium War (1856-1860) and the Indian Uprising (1857); and the worldwide recession of 1857.

Although today the Crimean War is of little interest compared to the World Wars, it intrigued those living at the time because it was the first major clash in 40 years after the Napoleonic Wars in the early 1800s. American audiences reveled in Marx's writings. Many of the military tactics articles were written by Engels and focused on the Siege of Sevastopol. Even though Marx disagreed with the Crimean invasion — he thought it was half-hearted — he still disagreed with the English capitalists who argued against the war because there were no economic gains.[98]

In addition to the Crimean War, which was more European focused, Marx also addressed topics and issues that pertained to the Orient. Like other 19th century German intellectuals and individuals, Marx was first introduced to the Orient through the Bible, which discussed the Babylonians, Persians, Mesopotamians, and others. It was even said that the Apostle Thomas ministered to those in India. When pondering with Engels the

---

96. McLellan, 2006.
97. Engels, 1993.
98. Sperber, 2013.

question of why the history of the Orient was the history of religion, Marx determined that the East included no private property and concluded "[t}his is the real key, even to oriental heaven."[99] Although Marx did not condone the British imperialists who emphasized the capitalistic benefits of colonialism, he did not argue against imperialism like Lenin. Instead, Marx believed, like Hegel, that change was not natural to Asian societies, although Marx did believe that Asian cultures could advance after an introduction to capitalism. Paradoxically, although colonialism certainly existed when Marx and his predecessors lived, it was not until the late 1880s that European imperialism really took off. I personally find this fact ironic because I often picture colonialism being a huge issue in the 1600s and 1700s.

 European countries acquired more colonies between 1850 to 1900 than in any other 56-year period in the history of the world.

Personal Tragedies

Personally, Marx struggled in the 1850s. Just two years after his second son Heinrich Guido died in infancy, Karl and Jenny's third daughter, Franziscka, was born on March 28, 1851 and died a little over a year later on April 14, 1852. They had a brief moment of happiness when their fourth daughter Eleanor was born on January 17, 1855, only to be followed by the death of Edgar, Musch or "little fly," from tuberculosis or a ruptured appendix. Edgar's death on April 6, 1855 was perhaps the greatest tragedy in Marx's life. Edgar's death deeply affected Marx because it was the death of his first son. In 1857 when Jenny was 43 years old, a stillborn child was born in July. Thus, in seven years, Karl and Jenny experienced the death of four children at Dean Street. While Jenny had given birth to six live children,

---

99. Sperber, 2013.

only three (the oldest girls, Jenny and Laura, and the youngest, Eleanor) would survive to adulthood.

Marx also had immense financial difficulties in the 1850s. In his estimation, 1852 was a particularly problematic period, as he had to borrow money to bury his daughter Franziscka.[100] Dr. McLellan suggests, however, that Marx's financial difficulties may have resulted from an intention to keep up appearances and maintain a certain lifestyle rather than suffering from real poverty. After all, Marx did have the regular income from serving as a correspondent for several newspapers, as well as receiving assistance from Engels.[101]

Additionally, on June 23, 1851, the Marx's maid, Helene Demuth, gave birth to a boy that many scholars have suggested was sired by Karl. Engels, perhaps in an attempt to preserve his friend's marriage, claimed to be the father of Frederick Lewis Demuth (1851-1929). Frederick was sent to a working class family in London and did not grow up with the Marx children, although Eleanor Marx later became acquainted with Frederick after her father's death and considered him a family friend. Some historians, however, disagree, arguing that there is not enough material to make the case that Frederick was Karl's son: "Since 1962 it has been claimed that Marx was the father of Helene Demuth's illegitimate son, but this is not well founded on the documentary materials available."[102] In any case, the 1850s were a trying time for Marx, regardless of whether he fathered an illegitimate child.

Although personally Marx experienced some difficulties in the 1850s and struggled to get involved in politics, his writing took off in the 1850s. In his day, Marx was much more well-known for his newspaper articles than

---

100. McLellan, 2006.
101. McLellan, 2006.
102. Carver, 1991.

his books, and his reputation during his day was probably the greatest in the 1850s. Known in America for his contributions to the *New York Tribune* and *Brumaire*, Marx made a name for himself. This is the Marx those living in the 19th century would have known, thus illustrating the importance of learning more about Marx and his life.

CHAPTER 8
London II 1859-1883

As Marx grew older, he became increasingly interested in capitalism and economic theory. In 1859, *A Contribution to the Critique of Political Economy*, a precursor for Marx's later *Das Kapital*. Eager to study more, Marx began investigating the political economy of the working class, which, as Engels noted in a newspaper article in 1868, discussed socialism in a scientific manner for the first time. Yet Marx did not publish anything pertaining to *Das Kapital* for two years. Given Marx's intense interest in studying political economy, he clearly had another task far more important: defending himself against defamation (the action of damaging someone's good reputation).

In the Northern Italian War of 1859, Napoleon III invaded the Austrian provinces of northern Italy. Some radicals welcomed the war because they believed it was a first step to Italian unification, while others thought it demonstrated French imperialism and urged for the intervention of other German states on Austria's side. Marx and Engels belonged to the latter. An anonymous pamphlet entitled *Po and Rhine*, sanctioned by Marx and written by Engels, argued that Napoleon III and the French were after the western regions of Germany and the areas around the Rhine River, and that the best defense was to defeat the French at the Po River in Italy. Just as Marx and Engels pondered how to publicize these thoughts, Wilhelm Liebknecht, a German socialist, urged Marx to take over the left-wing weekly newspaper *Das Volk* (*The People*) that was experiencing financial difficulties. Although Marx attempted to revitalize the newspaper by acquiring new subscribers and publishing a series of articles about the war of 1859, the paper ultimately failed by the end of August 1859.

Feud with Karl Vogt

The paper, however, did connect Marx with Karl Blind and influenced Marx's writing for two years. Blind was aware of Karl Vogt, a leading intellectual, prominent radical German political, materialist philosopher, and a professor of zoology who had emigrated from Switzerland. Vogt controversially supported the French invasion and called on Prussia to act in Germany as Piedmont had in Italy (which would later occur during German unification). Blind informed Marx that he believed Vogt was in the service of Napoleon III and likely composed a pamphlet with said assertions. Marx also passed along the information to Liebknecht who included doubts about Vogt's German allegiance in the *Augsburg General News*.

Vogt was enraged and published a short book attacking Marx because the former believed Marx had incited the attacks. Vogt's criticisms of Marx went beyond personal concerns and called into question Marx's political beliefs and the cause of social revolution. Marx refused to let someone else decimate his political and personal status, and attempted to restore his reputation by going to court, which found that Marx's case lacked sufficient evidence. Despite attempts to appeal the decision, the courts did not reconsider Marx's case against the two newspapers that had published material by Vogt against Marx, which Marx had called libel (a published false statement that is damaging to a person's reputation). As a last result, Marx composed *Herr Vogt*, in which Marx strongly defended his honor and reputation and responded to every claim leveled against him. Then Marx went further and laid out why he believed that Vogt was a paid agent of Napoleon III. One chapter in particular captures what Marx intended to communicate with *Herr Vogt*. Named after an Algerian author who supported French colonialism, the chapter was entitled "Da-Da Vogt" and described how Da-Da and Vogt both wanted to take over North Africa and the Rhineland. Historians seem divided on *Herr Vogt*: some consider it to be one of Marx's best works while others regard it as a poor use of time. In any case, Marx's speculations about Vogt working for the French government were correct as the new French republican government revealed in 1870 the secret correspondence and 50,000 franc payment between Napoleon III and Vogt. At least Marx had the pleasure of being proven right in his lifetime!

His honor now defended, Marx could turn his attention back to political economy — after he dealt with smallpox (a now-eradicated virus that used to be contagious, disfiguring, and often deadly) in his family. In November 1860, Jenny came down with the disease, and she and Karl quickly sent their daughters out of the house. Unsure if his wife would survive, Marx spent his time reading Darwin's *On the Origin of Species* and studying calculus to take his mind off of the difficulties. Although Jenny did survive smallpox, she retained facial scars from the illness for many years.[103]

 Although Marx did not live in America, he still held opinions on the American Civil War of 1861-1865. Both Engels and Marx supported the North and the anti-slavery cause. While Marx believed that the North would win out in the end due to a stronger economy and a greater population, Engels despaired that the Union might not have a strong enough military to defeat the South. In fact, Engels was impressed by the military prowess of many Con-

---

103. Sperber, 2013.

federate generals, in particular that of Stonewall Jackson, whom he called "the best guy in America."[104]

Political Changes in Germany

The death of Ferdinand Lassalle, who founded a labor party known as the General German Workers' Association, brought Marx back into the political current. Another act, though, had broader significance. A French organizer putting together a public meeting for workers in September 1864 asked Marx to recommend a German worker to speak. Marx suggested Johann Georg Eccarius.[105] That alone was not significant, but an action at the meeting was: the International Working Men's Association (IWMA), known later as the First International, was founded. Ever the manifesto writer, Marx was given the job of working on the statutes, which is now known as the "Inaugural Address."[106] Most prominently, the IWMA raised funds to support strikes throughout Europe from Berlin to Paris to Geneva. Although the IWMA was not a revolutionist, socialist, or communist organization, Marx still decided to back the organization because he believed such actions in favor of unions would eventually usher in the era of the communist revolution.

In addition to all of his political involvement, Marx still had time to bond with his family. In 1865, Laura, then 20 years old, recorded Marx's answers to a parlor game, which she entitled "Confessions of Marx." Laura's sister Jenny, then 21, also posed questions. Marx's favorite virtue overall was simplicity, while in a man, he preferred strength and in a woman, he favored weakness. Well aware of his abilities, Marx stated that his chief characteristic was singleness of purpose; except perhaps in finishing books! His idea of happiness was fighting while his idea of misery was submission. The vice he excused most was gullibility while he could not tolerate servility. His favorite occupation, as can be seen by the excessive

---

104. Sperber, 2013.
105. Sperber, 2013.
106. Sperber, 2013.

number of books he read, was book-worming. His favorite poets were Shake-speare, Aeschylus, and Goethe while Diderot was his favorite prose-writer. Marx's favorite heroes were Spartacus and Kepler while his favorite heroine came from Goethe's *Faust*, Gretchen. His favorite flower was daphne, and, unsurprisingly, his favorite color was red. Like a good father, Marx said that his favorite names were Laura and Jenny. Fish was his favorite dish. Finally, his favorite maxim translated as "nothing human is alien to me" while his favorite motto translated as "to doubt of everything."[107]

In the meantime, Prussia and the other German states experienced some significant changes. In an attempt to move toward unification of all the German states, Otto von Bismarck, the prime minister in Prussia, initiated war between Prussia and Austria in 1866. Many Germans feared that fighting between the German states would allow the French to come in and take over. In a move that surprised everyone, the Prussian army scored such a decisive victory over Austria — in just six weeks' time — that France under Louis Napoleon had no time to mobilize. Engels, the military expert, was extremely impressed.[108]

The Austro-Prussian War of 1866 — also known as the Seven Weeks' War, the Unification War, the Prussian-German War, the German Civil War, the War of 1866, the Brothers War, and the German War in Germany — featured Prussian-led German Confederation states against Austrian-led German Confederation states. With the Prussia victory, the power in the German states shifted from Austria to Prussia (remember how conservative Metternich had guided the balance of power in Europe?) and provided the impetus for later unification of all northern German states.

In 1867, Marx published the first volume of *Das Kapital*, the culmination of his study of political economy. He continued to research and write for this project until the end of his life. Although he did not complete any

---

107. Kamenka, 1983.
108. Sperber, 2013.

additional volumes, Engels assembled and published posthumously the re-maining two volumes.

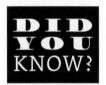 Marx saw the International as serving a specific purpose in bringing the working class together even if Marx would have liked to see more focus on communist ideals in the organization. As Marx stated in an interview in 1871, "[The International] is a network of affiliated societies spreading all over the world of labor ... Combinations among workmen cannot be absolutely identical in detail in Newcastle and in Barcelona, in London and in Berlin."[109]

From a political and activist side, Marx experienced some difficulties in the late 1860s. Although various radical groups from anarchists to socialists to communists differed in their beliefs, in the early to mid-1800s, they were able to get along fairly well. Even though he was frequently suspicious of Russia and the Russians, Marx had a high regard for well-known Russian anarchist Bakunin, writing to Engels in 1864 that Bakunin was "one of the few people who after 18 years has not gone backwards but has developed further."[110] In 1868, however, Marx and Bakunin disagreed about how to proceed with the IWMA. Bakunin wanted the International Alliance of Socialist Democracy, a secret society, to join the IWMA as an affiliated society. Marx had no desire for a clandestine organization to collaborate with the IWMA and convinced the General Council of the IWMA to ac-cept his opinions. Bakunin agreed that the secret society would have to be dissolved and that individual groups would enter separately. But the philo-sophical differences continued as Marx continued to dislike secret societies and Bakunin saw no issue with them. In fact, Marx attempted to arrange the 1870 Congress of the IWMA in Mainz in the German Rhineland be-cause Bakunin had little influence in that city.[111] It was not to be. Due to

---

109. Kamenka, 1983.
110. Sperber, 2013.
111. Sperber, 2013.

the recently begun war between Prussia and France that everyone had been expecting since 1866, the congress was never held.

Although Marx had originally been unsure of Bismarck's intentions to unify Germany, Bismarck's gamble paid off. When France declared war, it started a wave of nationalist sentiment, even from Karl and Jenny, who had always maintained a high regard for France and the French Revolution. In fact, Marx wrote to Engels, "The French need a thrashing."[112] Engels, on the other hand, equated the war with the nationalist uprising against Napoleon in 1813. The Franco-Prussian War ended in 1871 with a decisive victory for Prussia. Soon thereafter, Germany unified, all under the influence of Otto von Bismarck.

Helmut von Moltke, who oversaw the operation of the Schlieffen Plan of World War I in which Germany attempted to avoid a two-front war by winning a quick and decisive victory against France by entering through Belgium, played a major role in the Franco-Prussian War. Always appreciative of brilliant military strategy, Engels admired Moltke, the chief of the Prussian General Staff, and, swept in a wave of nationalism, the German soldiers. The Franco-Prussian War had significant repercussions. Germany took Alsace-Lorraine near the Rhineland from France, and France was itching to have those areas back, which eventually occurred after World War I. Many of the reasons that countries had for participating in World War I stemmed from the Franco-Prussian War.

Thus officially trounced, France wanted to sign a peace treaty with Prussia under Bismarck. The problem was that neither the French emperor, who was a prisoner of war, nor the French provisional republican government could sign a treaty. Bismarck allowed French elections, which were held in February 1871, and elected conservative monarchists. Many in Paris, however, disliked this decision, and the radicals proclaimed a revolutionary government known as the "Commune" on March 18, 1871. Per usual,

112. Sperber, 2013.

Marx had thoughts percolating in his head and wanted to respond to the recent events, especially given that he could read various newspapers in English, French, and German. Additionally, Marx had personal contacts with several leading figures and associates in the Commune, including Peter Lavrov and Paul Lafargue, who would later become Marx's son-in-law. Originally, Marx intended to compose an address to the workers in Paris, which the General Council of the International sanctioned, but later expanded his plan to address the working class of the world, also approved by the General Council. Thus, Marx wrote the pamphlet entitled "The Civil War in France" in May 1871. In the pamphlet, Marx praised the Paris Commune and called it a harbinger (a thing that announces or signals the approach of another or a forerunner of something) of the communist society to come.[113] By admiring the Paris Commune, Marx broke with many of those who composed the IWMA, including English trade unionists. As a result, Marx's political activism after 1871 began to decline, partly because of his increasing age.

 Marx had some interesting quirks. He loved telling stories to his three daughters and enjoyed reading. In an 1878 interview published in the *Chicago Tribune*, the author depicted Marx as an avid reader: "A man can generally be judged by the books he reads, and you can form your own conclusions when I tell you a casual glance revealed Shakespeare, Dickens, Thackeray, Molière, Racine, Montaigne, Bacon, Goethe, Voltaire, Paine; English, American, French bluebooks; works political and philosophical in Russian, German, Spanish, Italian, etc., etc."[114] This picture is not the one we would normally have of Marx! As several historians have noted, it is important to try to understand the 19th century world in which Marx lived instead of seeing him as a harbinger (a forerunner) of communist societies in the 20th century.

113. Sperber, 2013.
114. Kamenka, 1983.

The End of Marx's Life

In the 1870s, Marx's health began to decline. Marx was encouraged to go to Carlsbad, a fashionable spa on the river Egen in Bohemia (modern day Czech Republic) and went three straight years (1874-1876) in a row, sometimes with family and once on his own. In 1877, Marx went to a smaller spa in Neuenahr in the Rhineland because the cost of Carlsbad was simply too high.[115]

As Marx got older, he also saw his daughters marry. Two of them married Frenchmen. Amidst the happiness, the Marx family experienced even more tragedy. Just as four of Karl and Jenny's children had not survived infancy and childhood, Karl and Jenny's first four grandchildren did not live past infancy.

The late 1870s also brought several illnesses and deaths for Marx's family and close friends: Lizzie Burns, with whom Engels had lived since the death of Mary Burns, died of a tumor in her bladder, and Marx's wife Jenny was seriously ill with an incurable cancer.[116] Jenny's illness was so severe that she required constant attention, which Marx attempted to provide, thus ending his political career for good. By the middle of 1881, it was clear that Jenny was going to die soon. In October and November of that year, Marx himself suffered from bronchitis and could not visit his wife even though she was just a room away. The last days of November 1881 were especially painful for Jenny, but when she died on December 2, 1881, she died peacefully.[117] Jenny's death devastated Marx, and he never recovered. According to Engels, upon seeing Marx after Jenny's passing, the "Moor [Marx] is dead, too."[118]

---

115. McLellan, 2006.
116. McLellan, 2006.
117. McLellan, 2006.
118. McLellan, 2006.

In 1882, Marx traveled a far amount with his daughters to Ventnor, Algiers, and Argenteuil. In late 1882 and early 1883, Marx's daughter Jennychen suffered just like her mother, presumably from a type of cancer in the bladder, and on January 11, 1883, Jennychen died at the age of 38. The death of his first-born child as well as his wife in roughly a year overwhelmed Marx, and he remarked on Jennychen's death, "our Jennychen is dead."[119] Marx's homecoming trip to London would be his last, and many believe that he returned to London to die.

In early 1883, Marx's reading had subsided. He read only catalogues and occasionally French novels when desiring something more intellectually stimulating. Marx had an ulcer in his lung, irritating and complicating his bronchitis, but the doctor believed if Marx could survive two cold winter months, Marx would have several more years of good life ahead. And Marx's condition did improve slightly. On March 14, 1883, however, Engels's daily visit suddenly turned into mourning. When he visited in the afternoon, Laura, who had been taking care of her father, noted that Marx had experienced a small hemorrhage and his condition had deteriorated. When Laura had last seen Marx, he was half-asleep, but when Engels went in to see his friend, Marx had already passed away peacefully, quietly, and painlessly.

Marx died of pleurisy — an inflammation of the pleurae that is caused by pneumonia and similar diseases and impairs the lubricating function of the pleurae and causes pain when breathing — on March 14, 1883 in London. His original grave included only a small stone, which the Communist Party of Great Britain updated with a large tombstone, featuring a bust of Marx, in 1956. The 11th theses from Marx's *Theses on Feuerbach* as well as the last line of *The Communist Manifesto* — "Workers of the world, unite!" — are etched on the tombstone.

---

119. McLellan, 2006.

On March 17, 1883, Engels gave a short eulogy for Marx at Highgate Cemetary to only 10 other people. The man who Engels called "the greatest living thinker" did not seem to have much of a following. It was not until years later that Marx would rise in prominence, becoming one of the most recognizable names of the 1900s.

CHAPTER 9
Major Works

❧ *The Jewish Question, The Communist Manifesto, and Das Kapital* ☙

Marx may have been a prolific newspaper writer during his lifetime, but he is more well-known for his books, three of which are particularly famous: *The Jewish Question*, *The Communist Manifesto*, and *Das Kapital*.

The Jewish Question

Although slightly less well-known than the other two works, *The Jewish Question* is interesting because it illustrates Marx's first attempts to develop a materialist conception of history, as well as addressing the role of Jews in society. Given that some totalitarian states in the 20th century were extremely anti-Semitic, Marx's thoughts on Jews are worth considering. Marx's former idol Bruno Bauer had written a book published in 1843 that discussed the Jewish attempt to achieve political emancipation in Prussia. In the same year, Marx began his own book in response to Bauer's, agreeing with Bauer in critiquing the state, but suggesting that Bauer still focused too much on civil emancipation.

According to Marx, man needed to recognize himself as more social and less egotistical. In other words, Marx wanted people to focus more on others and less on themselves. Marx wanted to see philosophy turned into action or revolution, which he believed would occur in Germany. Marx thought that Germany was behind France in politics, but not in philosophy (note, for example, the Reformation). France had long been Catholic, but Germany was willing to break with tradition and make some changes to doctrinal issues through the Reformation, which Marx believed was philosophically forward. Marx saw this distinction as important because he believed that philosophy guided politics.

While Bauer wanted to abolish religion for true political emancipation, Marx believed that did not go far enough. Economic inequality had to be addressed before individuals could be completely free from the state. Even so, Marx did believe that religion was an arm of the Prussian government and represented alienation, invoking Hegelian rhetoric that emphasized Reason and Progress.

Some historians consider sections of *The Jewish Question* as anti-Semitic, but given Marx's other interactions and relations with Jews, it seems likely that he just utilized the language of his day, not necessarily in a derogatory way. It should also be noted, however, that Marx did sometimes make anti-Jewish remarks and never identified with his ethnic, cultural, and religious heritage, although his daughter Eleanor would later make the famous comment, "I am a Jewess." Even so, Marx was also willing to help Jews in Cologne, so when he utilized the word *Judentum*, meaning either Jewry or commerce, it seems likely that Marx referred to Jews who had popularized capitalism, not necessarily Jews as a whole.[120] In other words, Marx seemed to dislike Jews who propagated capitalism, but he did not have an antipathy for all Jews.

---

120. McLellan, 2006.

 While Marx disliked religion because it separated man from material society, he did appreciate that Christianity had taught him (and others) to love children. Even so, Marx considered atheism a key component of communism. An individual would continue to be alienated and separated from society and from himself or herself until he or she moved beyond religion to materialism and humanism.[121]

The Communist Manifesto

Probably all that you know about Marx comes from reading some excerpts of *The Communist Manifesto* in an English or history class. You likely know that Marx and Engels wrote the manifesto in 1848 and that Marx later spelled out communism more in *Das Kapital*. Marx's famous work utilized Hegelian logic and illustrated class struggle throughout the ages. According to Marx, capitalism increased the gap between the rich and the poor. Nonetheless, communism under the proletariat will be triumphant. Marx believed the main drive would come from the industrial workers and that the revolution would occur in Germany. He was wrong, however, as we know the revolution took place in Russia in 1917. From that date until the collapse of the Soviet Union in 1991, communism played a prominent role in the world.

The work itself is divided into a preamble and four sections. The introduction notes that a spectre (or ghost) is haunting Europe — the ghost of communism. All types of individuals from conservatives like Klemens von Metternich of Austria to French radicals have tried to get rid of this ghost. Marx and Engels present the manifesto as an opportunity to state openly the principles of the party, which they delineate in the following sections:

---

121. McLellan, 2006.

The Communist Manifesto, a guide book about communism.

1. Bourgeois and Proletarians

2. Proletarians and Communists

3. Socialist and Communist Literature

4. Position of the Communists in relation to the various existing Opposition Parties

The Communist Manifesto famously ends with the following words:

> The Communists disdain to conceal their views and aims. They openly declare that their ends can be attained only by the forcible overthrow of all existing social conditions. Let the ruling classes tremble at a Communistic revolution. The proletarians have nothing to lose but their chains. They have a world to win. Working-men of all countries unite![122]

Marx and Engels entitled their work *The Communist Manifesto* and not *The Socialist Manifesto* because they wanted to distinguish themselves from less radical forms of socialism. Marx and Engels advocated for a complete reordering of society, including the famous component of the abolition of private property. In addition, they also wanted a heavy progressive or graduated income tax, abolition of all rights of inheritance, confiscation of the property of all emigrants and rebels, centralization of credit in the hands of the state, centralization of the means of communication and transportation, extension of factories and instruments of production owned by the state, equal obligation of all to work, combination of agriculture with manufacturing industries, and free education for all children in government schools. In order to bring out such a communist society, Marx and Engels believed that there had to be a revolution, likely accompanied by violence. According to Marx, communism could only achieve its ends through forcible overthrow.

---

122. Marx, 2011.

Das Kapital

In *Das Kapital*, Marx further developed his economic and political philosophy. Because the value of a product was determined by the amount of labor that produced it, laborers were the creators of value, rather than the capitalist factory owners. Marx believed that capitalism would increasingly be controlled by the few, requiring the workers to revolt and produce a classless society where the workers could rule themselves. The first volume was published in Berlin in 1867; the second and third were edited by Engels and published posthumously in 1885 and 1894, respectively.

 Marx's biographer Francis Wheen believes that *Das Kapital* reads like a Gothic novel (a genre or mode of literature and film that combines fiction and horror, death, and at times romance). According to Wheen, *Das Kapital* is a novel "whose heroes are enslaved and consumed by the monster they created."[123]

Unlike liberals of his day who worried about the role of a larger population on the economy, Marx believed that large unemployment caused by capitalists drove wages to subsistence level. Because capitalist bosses could force workers to labor past wages needed to live, the former acquired the surplus value, which Marx considered an exploitation of labor. Since workers do not own the products of their labor, they are little better than machines, making an economic system based on private property, like capitalism, inherently unstable. Marx believed that it was inevitable that capitalist society would collapse on its own, but he did not detail what a communist society that replaced a capitalist society would look like. It is important to note, however, that Marx died before completing all that he had planned for *Das Kapital* so perhaps he intended to expound on communist society.

---

123. Wheeler, 2017.

CHAPTER 10
Lasting Significance and Legacy

⚔ *"A Not Very Important 19th Century Philosopher"* ⚔

Marx's Children

As previously noted, only three of the Marx children survived childhood: Jenny, Laura, and Eleanor. All of Marx's daughters took after their father and were politically active. Two of them, Jenny and Laura, married Frenchmen. Both their husbands became prominent French socialists and members of Parliament.

In 1870 the eldest, Jenny Caroline Marx (later Longuet), briefly served as a political journalist under the pen name of "J. Williams" and discussed the treatment of Irish political prisoners. Her work did have some effect on the investigation of the Irish government under William Gladstone.[124] For the rest of her short life, she taught language classes and helped raise a family of five children before dying at the age of 38.

---

124. "Jenny Marx Longuet (Jennychen)."

 Benjamin Disraeli (Dizzy) and William Gladstone (the Grand Old Man) politically dominated the Victorian Age (1837-1901) in England. Both served as Prime Minister in Britain. Gladstone was well-versed in the classics, mathematics, and theology and was highly intellectual (he spent spare moments during his honeymoon reading Greek and Latin texts), and he desired a moral force in politics. He leaned conservative, and Augustine, Dante, Burke, and Canning were some of his favorite authors. Additionally, Gladstone was known for his eloquent and abundant speeches. Regarding Ireland, Gladstone attempted to address the Irish concerns pertaining to land, religion, and home rule. In the late 1800s, Gladstone companioned two land acts that would give Irish landowners less power and benefit the tenants. Since many in Ireland were Catholic, Gladstone disestablished the Protestant Church of Ireland. Finally, Gladstone encouraged home rule and championed two home bills in the late 1800s that were not passed. In the end, however, Gladstone was right on the Irish question as Ireland achieved qualified independence in 1920-1921.

The second oldest, Jenny Laura Marx, known simply as Laura, became politically active after she married French socialist Paul Lafargue. In 1866, Lafargue went to London to work for the First International, become friends with Karl Marx and his family, and later developed a relationship with Laura. The two married in 1868 and began political work together. They translated Marx's works into French and helped spread Marxism in Spain and France. On November 25, 1911, Laura and Paul committed suicide together, having decided that they had completed their life work and did not need to live past 70. They were 66 and 69 respectively.

Interestingly, Vladimir Lenin spoke at the funeral of Paul and Laura Lafargue on November 20, 1911, noting how much the Lafargues had contributed to the Russian Social Democratic Party:

"Even in the period of preparation for the Russian revolution, the class-conscious workers and all Social-Democrats of Russia learned profound respect for Lafargue as one of the most gifted and profound disseminators of the ideas of Marxism, ideas that were so

brilliantly confirmed by the class struggle during the Russian revolution and counter-revolution."[125]

The famous Russian Revolution of 1917 had not yet occurred. The less
famous Russian Revolution of 1905, however, had spread a wave of political and social unrest throughout the Russian Empire, including strikes and
mutinies. While the change that resulted from the 1905 Revolution was
less radical than the 1917 Revolution, constitutional reform did ensue,
including the establishment of the Russian Constitution of 1906 and the
founding of the State Duma, which means "State Assembly" in Russian.

Jenny Julia Eleanor Marx, also known as Tussy to the family and known to
outsiders as Eleanor, was the youngest. She was a socialist activist and literary translator, including the first translation of Gustave Flaubert's *Madame
Bovary*. As Eleanor grew up, Marx had been working on *Das Kapital*, so she
had a close connection with that work; she translated and edited volumes
of *Das Kapital* as an adult. Marx had even told Eleanor before he died that
he wanted her to publish his manuscripts and the English version of *Das
Kapital*, which Eleanor did oversee after Engels's death. Rachel Holmes,
Eleanor Marx's biographer, believes that had it not been for Eleanor, the
modern world would not know as much as about Karl Marx and his
writings.

Holmes also asserts that Eleanor did more as a woman to transform British
politics than anyone else. In 1884, she joined the Social Democratic Fed-
eration (SDF) where she met Edward Aveling, a man with whom she would
spend the rest of her life. In addition to writing regularly for *Commonweal*,
the Socialist League's monthly newspaper in a column entitled "Record of
the Revolutionary International Movement," Eleanor also helped organize
the International Socialist Congress in Paris in 1885 and traveled to the

125. Lenin, 1974.

United States with Aveling and German socialist Wilhelm Liebknecht to raise money for the Social Democratic Party of Germany. In the late 1880s, the Socialist League divided over how much involvement to have with the government. Eleanor and her lover Aveling were in the minority (who advocated for more involvement in political campaigns) and briefly were a part of the minority branch, the Bloomsbury Socialist Society. However, they later rejoined the SDF as many others had done, likely because their attempts to join other political parties and turn them toward Marxism were unsuccessful.

In late March 1898, sometime between March 27 and March 31, Eleanor discovered that Aveling had secretly married a young actress in July 1897, Eva Frye. Eleanor was devastated, and she had a fight with Aveling the morning of March 31, according to her housekeeper Gertrude Gentry. During the mid-morning, Eleanor sent her maid on an errand to acquire chloroform and prussic acid (hydrogen cyanide) for the dog, signed by E.A., the initials of her lover who was a doctor and often requested medicines. In the late afternoon of March 31, Gertrude found Eleanor dead in her room, wearing her favorite white summer dress, and her body completely changed to the color purple. Although the coroner decided that Eleanor had a spell of madness that caused her to commit suicide through poison, within three weeks after her death, Eleanor's family, friends, and political allies accused Aveling of murder. He died of kidney disease within four months of Eleanor and never faced a trial.

Eleanor was deeply mourned, much more so than her father. Letters of condolence and obituaries filled European society in languages Eleanor did not even know existed. When the Marx Memorial Library opened in 1933, 50 years after Marx's death, Eleanor's ashes were placed in the Lenin Room.

In 1956, when the gravesite of Karl Marx received a renovation, Eleanor's urn was placed in the family grave and her birth date, which was incorrect, and her death date, which was correct, was carved in the tombstone.[126]

 Marx was close with all of his daughters. When Eleanor Marx reflected back on growing up in the Marx household with her father, she speaks very fondly of him. Referring to her father as "Mohr" (the Moor), she noted, "Mohr was not only an excellent horse, but (a still higher commendation) a unique and unrivalled story-teller."[127] Eleanor also remembered the books Marx read to his daughters:

> "To me, as to my sisters, he read the whole of Homer [*Iliad* and *Odyssey*], the Nibelungenlied [a poem in Middle High German about a dragon-slayer and his wife's revenge], Gudrun [a major figure in early Germanic literature], Don Quixote, The Thousand and One Nights. Shakespeare was our family Bible and before I was six I knew whole scenes of Shakespeare by heart."[128]

Reading was clearly important to Marx, and he passed that love to his children. Eleanor also remembered her father's opinions on Christianity. The family would occasionally go to Catholic churches to hear music, and Marx did tell the story of Jesus to his children, focusing more to the poor and rich aspect as opposed to the spiritual ramifications. While Marx certainly did not believe that Jesus was the Son of God, he still liked the morals of Christianity: "Often and often I heard him say: 'After all, we can forgive Christianity much, since it taught us to love children.'"[129] Finally, Eleanor reflected back on her youth and deemed her father "an ideal friend."[130]

126. Holmes, 2014.
127. Kamenka, 1983.
128. Kamenka, 1983.
129. Kamenka, 1983.
130. Kamenka, 1983.

Spokespeople for Marx's Ideals

When Marx died, Engels became the spokesperson and disseminator of Marx's works. Scholars debate how closely Engels held true to Marx's ideals. It is likely fair to say that Engels may have overemphasized positivism (a philosophy that certain or positive knowledge can only come from the senses, but not from abstract theories), a belief to which Engels held but Marx was more ambivalent. But the evidence does suggest that Engels was as fair as possible to Marx. For example, Engels noted in a letter, "What I pay most attention to is to publish a true edition of Marx's works with all my heart, in other words, we must use Marx's texts to the full to express his own discoveries."[131] Because Engels was a close friend of Marx for many years, it is likely that he stayed as true as possible to his old friend. Additionally, Marx was not a household name until the success of the Russian Revolution of 1917, and Engels would not have much to gain from intentionally misrepresenting Marx. Quite frankly, most people would not have even recognized Marx's name.

When Engels died in 1895, Eleanor, who had become involved in the Social Democratic Party, oversaw the publication of some of Marx's letters under the auspices of the party. From 1895 to 1914, the Social Democratic Party was the main publisher of Marx's writings and published unknown writings as well as reprinted other important writings.[132] The main influx of publication, however, took place in the pre-Soviet Marx-Engels Institute under Riazanov. As Zou and Yang note, "[l]ess than one-third of Marx's writings were published or took shape during his lifetime, with enormous remainders of notes, letters, reading notes, annotations, and commentaries which were not published or finished."[133] The Pre-Soviets, however, did

---

131. Zou and Yang, 2007.
132. Zou and Yang, 2007.
133. Zou and Yang, 2007.

have a strong understanding of their own social ideology, which certainly informed their reading of Marx.

The most recent (and now the definitive) publications of Marx's work come from *MEGA* (Marx-Engels-Gesamtausgabe), the largest collection of the works of Marx and Engels. Founded in 1958, *MEGA* contains material written by Marx between 1835 and 1883 (his death) and by Engels between 1838 and 1895 (his death). All the material is in German, and the complete works is expected to exceed 110 volumes. Many historians consider *MEGA* to be the best source of Marx's works, as it was developed to understand Marx better and not to advance a certain agenda.

The Russian Revolution and the Soviet Union

Up until the Russian Revolution of 1917, communism had not succeeded. In February, the Russians overthrew 300 years of czar rule for a democratic government.

A czar is a Russian ruler or emperor of Russia from the 1500s until the Russian Revolution of 1917. Czars were absolute monarchs, meaning they had supreme authority and normally were not bound by written laws or a legislature. Czar can also be spelled tsar.

In October, the Russians overthrew the democratic government for a communist one. After five years of war between the Reds and Whites, Vladimir Ilich Lenin, a follower of Marx, organized the Soviet Union as a proletarian dictatorship based on Lenin's interpretations of Marx's works. Although Marx certainly had some prominence in the 1800s, it was not until the success and controversy of the Soviet Union that Marx and his works became known worldwide.

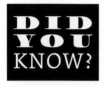

The Whites were a loosely connected group of anti-communists that fought the communist Bolsheviks, also known as the Reds, in the Russian Civil War of 1917 to 1922. Since the French Revolution of 1789, red has been the symbolic color of revolution while white has symbolized royalty.

As Alan Ryan suggests, without Lenin and the Soviet Union, Marx would never have the recognition that he maintains now: "If the German government had not sent Lenin across its territory and back to Russia in a sealed train in early 1917, we might today regard Marx as a not very important 19th century philosopher, sociologist, economist, and political theorist."[134] Ironically, the Russians that Marx so disliked actually ended up making him famous.

Nowadays Marxism is often referred to in connection with Leninism: Marxist-Leninism, which is slightly different from Marx's original ideas. While Lenin accepted many of Marx and Engels' ideas, he did adapt them to suit the Soviet Union's needs. Hence, when the phrase "Marxist-Leninism" is used, it indicates Marx's beliefs as interpreted by Lenin.

Even so, Lenin altered some of Marx's beliefs and dogmas. Lenin believed that Marx's thoughts were somewhat fluid and could be interpreted as needed for action. As one example, Marx and Engels believed that the communist society would come from the working class while Lenin believed that professional revolutionaries would bring about the communist society.

Although Russia had been the backward country of Europe for many years (for example, Russia did not abolish serfdom (person in servitude, which was very common in the Middle Ages) until 1861), Lenin was able to radicalize the government due to failures with Czar Nicholas II and the Provi-

---

134. Ryan, 2014.

sional Government. Russia entered World War I (then known as the Great War) in 1914, but had experienced devastating losses against the Germans on the Eastern Front. The czar seemed detached from the Russian people, and by 1917, famine had swept across the entire country. The people clamored for food and new leaders. In March 1917, after riots in Petrograd (formerly St. Petersburg), the czar abdicated (gave up his throne) on March 15 to his brother Grand Duke Michael, who refused the crown and thus ended over 300 years of the ruling Romanov Dynasty. At first, they turned to a democratic-parliamentary government called the Provisional Government, appointed by the Duma (the Russian Legislature), but this body was extremely weak. Its rival, the Petrograd Soviet of Workers' and Soldiers' Deputies, was more closely connected to the people due to its presence in cities, towns, and the army. The Soviet slogan of "peace, land, and bread" continued to acquire more support from the people, and the Soviets (largely Bolsheviks) staged a practically bloodless coup on November 6-7 and occupied government buildings and other strategic. Soon thereafter, the Provisional Government, reorganized four times between March and November 1917, was replaced with a communist system, headed originally by Lenin until 1924 when Josef Stalin replaced him.

Animal Farm is Orwell's critique of the Russian Revolution. Orwell was a Socialist and felt that those who grouped Communism under Socialism were wrong and that the USSR had greatly deviated from the true principles of Socialism. Orwell explicitly states that he used events from the Russian Revolution and beyond in his story, so understanding his references will greatly enrich a student's comprehension of Animal Farm as well as the Russian Revolution and early Soviet history.

By World War II, the Soviet Union under Stalin had become an extremely powerful nation. Many of the other nations of Europe had been devastated by the fighting and Nazi occupation, so the Soviet Union and the United States emerged as the economically and politically strongest countries.

While the Soviet Union under Stalin and the United States under Franklin D. Roosevelt and later Harry S. Truman had been allies during World War II, their close connection fizzled away in the 1950s, and a new conflict that did not have any official "hot" confrontations between the two nations occurred: the Cold War. For many, this new 'war' represented two conflicting ideologies (capitalism and communism), and the question was: which one was better? In the end, capitalism outlasted communism when the Berlin Wall was taken down in 1989 and the Soviet Union dissolved in 1991.

Perhaps one of the starkest comparisons of communism and capitalism occurred in Germany, which had been divided after World War II at the Potsdam Conference of July 17 to August 2, 1945. Germany was originally separated into four zones: France in the southwest, Britain in the northwest, the United States in the south, and the Soviet Union in the east. In 1949, two states emerged; one was a conglomeration of the Allied zones (the Federal Republic of Germany, also known as West Germany) while the other was under the influence of the Soviets (the German Democratic Republic, also known as East Germany). The former was a parliamentary democracy with a capitalist economy while the latter was a Marxist-Leninist socialist republic. Even Germany's capital, Berlin, was divided into two zones: West Berlin governed by the Allies and East Berlin controlled by the Soviet Union. Because too many East Germans were escaping to Western Germany to enjoy the benefits of a capitalist society through West Berlin, the communist East German authorities constructed a wall that totally encircled West Berlin in one night on August 13, 1961, known as the Berlin Wall. From 1961 to 1989 when the wall was taken down, West Berlin (and West Germany) and East Berlin (and East Germany) provided a contrast between capitalism and communism: the former continued to prosper while the latter was ugly and grim.

 Capitalism is an economic and political system in which trade and industry are controlled by the private industry. Communism is a political and economic system in which property and resources are collectively owned by a classless society and each person works and is paid according to his or her abilities and needs.

Marx's Legacy

Many of the most atrocious deeds in the 20th century were the result of communist dictators, so one has to question if such actions were continuations of Marx's thoughts or deviations from it. In many cases, the communist dictators diverged from Marx's original plans and programs. For example, Pol Pot and the Khmer Rouge (the name given to the followers of the Communist Party of Kampuchea) tried to implement a type of agrarian communism in Cambodia from 1975 to 1979. The totalitarian government moved city dwellers to the countryside to work in collective farms and work camps: a communist ideal of government controlling the means of production in a classless society. While Marx did advocate for violence to bring about the communist revolution, he never intended for the genocide that happened in Cambodia. Between 1.5 and 3 million Cambodians (almost 25 percent of the total population of Cambodia) died in four years at the hand of Pol Pot and the Khmer Rouge through disease, forced labor, malnutrition, mass executions, and torture. Pol Pot's policies differed so greatly from Marx's original intent that many communists today refuse to consider the Khmer Rouge as a communist government. *The Killing Farms*, a 1984 British movie about the Khmer Rouge regime in Cambodia, depicts these atrocities and is based on the experiences of two journalists: Cambodian Dith Pran and American Sydney Schanberg.

 Many historians debate who killed more people: Hitler and the Nazis or Stalin and the Communists. Recent archival information suggests that it was Hitler and the Germans, who killed about 11 million civilians while Stalin and the Soviets killed somewhere between six and nine million noncombatants. As Timothy Snyder noted, "These figures are of course subject to revision, but it is very unlikely that the consensus will change again as radically as it has since the opening of Eastern European archives in the 1990s."[135] Snyder does note, however, that until World War II, Stalin and the Soviets killed far more people. It was not until after the Molotov-Ribbentrop Pact and the joint Nazi-Soviet invasion of Poland in 1939 that Nazi Germany started to match the killing levels of the Soviet Union in their termination of civilians and noncombatants.[136] It should be noted, however, that neither of these numbers include the numbers of soldiers that died as a result of World War II.

Marx is perhaps most known for his approach to history and economics. In history, Marx believed only materialism mattered while in economics, Marx argued for replacing greedy capitalism, the stage before communism, with a proletariat revolution. No matter one's opinion on communism, Marx certainly has influenced the study of history as he has his own school of history: Marxism.

Karl Marx even had an influence outside of communism, Marxism, and other radical ideas. Even those who do not completely support communism or Marxism often suggest some sort of mixture between communism and the free market, such as democratic socialism, managed capitalism, market socialism, and welfare capitalism.

---

135. Snyder, 2011.
136. Snyder, 2011.

Democratic Socialism	A political ideology that encourages democracy alongside socialism. Often, democratic socialism proposes democracy in politics and socialism in economics (although the government does not necessarily own the means of production). Public schools, military, fire department, police department, and public roads are all socialized matters, mainly due to cost reasons.
Managed Capitalism	An economic system in which the government controls commercial economic activity and the means of production are managed by state-owned businesses. It is also known as state capitalism.
Market Socialism	An economic system in which the government controls the means of production, but the production is not centrally planned and instead is mediated by the market. Also known as liberal socialism, market socialism blends public ownership with a market economy.
Welfare Capitalism	A political ideology concerned with the welfare of workers provided by private businesses. Largely utilized in the twentieth century, welfare capitalism believes that private businesses can provide better welfare programs than the federal government. It is often juxtaposed to the welfare state.

Conclusion

Although not a household name in the 1800s, Karl Marx would rise to prominence after the First World War and even more so after the Second World War. His name and ideals would be known from the United States to Russia to China to even Germany, where Marx and Engels first imagined the communist revolution. Marx's vision of the world, one where each man would not be chained to a task but could be a student in the morning, an accountant in the afternoon, and a physical therapist in the evening revolutionized modern-day politics. While the communist governments of the 20th century likely went beyond Marx's conception of a communist society, they did inherit and pass on Marx's focus on the workers, how such people could oust the ruling class, and how to oppose capitalism.

Even today in non-communist countries like the United States, Marx's emphasis on the worker is felt. "Workers of the world, unite!" is a common sentiment throughout the world. For example, the Occupy Wall Street movement of 2011 utilized a slogan very similar to Marx's quip at the end of *The Communist Manifesto*: "We are the 99 percent." In many respects, the Occupy movement shared Marx's concerns about capitalism: the wealthiest people in society have a disproportionate share of capital, political influence, and means of production. Like Marx, the movement wants workers and the middle class — the 99 percent — to have more influence and capital. Unlike Marx, however, the Occupy movement did not advocate a completely communist society in which private property is abolished and the government controls the means of production.

Karl Marx is a difficult figure. It's important to understand Marx in his 19th century context while at the same time recognizing the ramifications Marxism had in the 20th century and beyond. While you might not want "Workers of the world, unite!" engraved on your tombstone or desire a communist society, hopefully this book has taught you more about Karl Marx and his famous pamphlet, *The Communist Manifesto*.

Author's Note/Acknowledgements

While people may think that they understand Karl Marx, they are likely wrong. Given the prominent role the Soviet Union played in the 20th century, terms like Marxist-Leninism and Communism are used every day. Comics and cartoons of Marx abound, and Karl Marx (like another namesake, Groucho Marx!) is a name recognized by many people. Communist countries have invoked Marx's tenets regularly, and *The Communist Manifesto* is required reading in many high schools and college. But how much would Marx approve of the superfluity of communist governments in the 20th century? Would Marx support the violence that they used, or have they gone beyond Marx's original idea? How well do modern individuals even understand *The Communist Manifesto*? For example, my students did not realize that at the end of *The Communist Manifesto*, Marx and Engels include a comment about how they believed the proletariat revolution would begin in Germany. Of course, it actually occurred in Russia as a direct result of the czar's mismanagement of World War I. Facts like this one help put Marx back in his context.

Writing a book is always a difficult, although enjoyable, project. I would like to especially thank several groups of people who provided encouragement every step of the way. Danielle Lieneman and everyone at Atlantic Publishing Group were always extremely helpful. Danielle and I share a common interest in history, so I enjoyed checking in with her as the book developed. Of course, I'm grateful to my students who are always willing to be guinea pigs when I try out new ideas. This past school year (2016-2017), I spent quite a bit of time on Karl Marx, Marxism, and *The Communist Manifesto*, and my students always asked great questions that helped me deepen my thoughts about Marx (and were eager for the book to come out!). I would like to especially thank Evan and Cole Frazier, two of my former students, who regularly talked with me about Communism and Marxism after school. Their eagerness to understand this ideology prompted me to study more about Marx and Communism. Christian Urch, another former student and current history major at a local college, took a class on Stalinist Russia and was especially helpful in assisting with any question I had about communism or the Soviet Union. As always, Gil and Carolyn Petrina offered encouragement and insights every step of the way. My best friend, Sair Wagner, was extremely energetic about my project and was excited to finally be able to buy them. I would also like to thank especially my college roommate, Megan Korpics, who assisted me with better understanding the German words Marx used. I am also extremely grateful to Dr. Matthew Gaetano for first helping me to really understand Marx (and also Darwin) in one of my final college classes, Western Heritage 2. Finally, I am thankful for my supportive family (my parents, Gary and LaRue, and my sister and brother-in-law, Rebekah and Daniel) who regularly asked about my progress and would give me suggestions along the way. As an editor, Rebekah has copyedited quite a number of works about Jews in Eastern Europe, so we talked a fair amount about how to discuss certain topics that are much debated in historical scholarship (like Hitler's conflation of Jews with Bolsheviks) and how to best handle those topics in a balanced and nuanced way. Rebekah has certainly been the person most excited about my book, and that was always encouraging.

Reading outside of school is incredibly important. I would encourage you to follow whatever in this book strikes your fancy. If a fact you really enjoyed has a footnote, check out the book that I cited in the library. I personally especially enjoyed reading several books in preparation to write this book about Karl Marx. The Very Short Introductions published by Oxford University Press are always excellent, and the one about Karl Marx by Peter Singer was no exception. Jonathan Sperber's *Karl Marx: A Nineteenth-Century Life* was superb and ought to be the definitive work on Karl Marx. David McLellan's *Karl Marx: A Biography* is also worth reading as it has been the definitive English biography of Marx since the 1970s. I am grateful to my sister Rebekah for loaning me her copy of *The Communist Manifesto* (she was so generous that I can use it until July 20, 2030 — there is a note in the front of the book) and would highly recommend that you read this short, definitive work. It is a primary source that will give you a good idea of Marx's political opinions. From there, you can also read other manifestos that have invoked the original, such as The Humanist Manifesto and the Feminist Manifesto. (For those Star Wars fans out there, Grand Moff Tarkin's comment in Rogue One — "We need a statement, not a manifesto" — is certainly redolent (suggestive) of *The Communist Manifesto*.) If you are interested in learning more about the ramifications of Marxism in the Soviet Union, George Orwell's *Animal Farm* is certainly the place to start. I am planning to teach the Russian Revolution this year using *Animal Farm* because Orwell stated directly that *Animal Farm* describes the details of the Russian Revolution (so I am not blue-curtaining to try to find something that is not there). I would urge you to see how the pig character, Napoleon, is Stalin, the Battle of Cowshed stood for the Russian Civil War, and how the meeting at the end between the humans and pigs represented the Tehran Conference of 1943. Old Major in *Animal Farm* delivers a speech that sounds similar to the *Communist Manifesto*. See if you can spot the correspondences!

Historical Timeline

5 May 1918	Karl Marx is born to Heinrich and Henriette Marx in Trier
28 November 1820 – 5 August 1895	Life of Friedrich Engels
October 1935	Marx enrolls at Bonn University as a law student
Summer 1836	Marx proposes to Jenny von Westphalen
22 October 1836	Marx enrolls as a law student at University of Berlin after a year at the University of Bonn
15 April 1841	Marx receives a doctorate of Philosophy from University of Jena
15 October 1842 – 18 March 1843	Marx serves as editor-in-chief of the *Rhineland News*
19 June 1843	Marx marries Jenny von Westphalen
February 1844	The first and last issue of the *German-French Yearbooks* is published
1 May 1844 – 11 January 1883	Life of Jenny Marx (first daughter of Karl and Jenny)
February 1845	*The Holy Family* is published

26 September 1845 – 25 November 1911	Life of Laura Marx (second daughter of Karl and Jenny)
September 1845 – Summer 1846	Marx and Engels work on *The German Ideology*
3 February 1847 – 6 April 1855	Life of Edgar Marx (first son of Karl and Jenny)
July 1847	*Poverty of Philosophy* is published in French in Brussels
29 November – 8 December 1847	Second Congress of the Communist League
February 1848	*The Communist Manifesto* published
5 November 1849 – 19 November 1850	Life of Heinrich Guido Marx (second son of Karl and Jenny)
28 March 1851 – 14 April 1852	Life of Franziska Marx (third daughter of Karl and Jenny)
December 1851 – March 1852	Marx writes *The Eighteenth Brumaire of Louis Bonaparte*
16 January 1855 – 31 March 1898	Life of Eleanor Marx (fourth daughter of Karl and Jenny)
11 June 1859	*A Contribution to the Critique of Political Economy*, Part One is published
14 September 1867	*Das Kapital*, Volume I is published
2 December 1881	Jenny Marx dies
14 March 1883	Karl Marx dies in London and is buried at Highgate Cemetery

Glossary

Anti-Semitic: Hostility to or prejudice against Jews

Bolshevik: Literally meaning "one of the majority" in contrast to Menshevik (a faction of the Russian socialist movement that emerged in 1904), Bolshevik indicated a member of the majority faction of the Russian Social Democratic Party who agreed with Lenin that capitalism needed to be overthrown. After the October Revolution of 1917, the Bolsheviks of the Russian Social Democratic Party became the Communist Party.

Bourgeoisie: A French term that originally meant those from the borough or city, bourgeoisie became a derogatory term due to Marx's division of society into two class: the bourgeoisie and the proletariat. In contrast to the proletariat class, which is focused on earning wages and is the poorer class, the bourgeoisie is primarily concerned with property values.

Capitalism: An economic and political system in which trade and industry are controlled by the private industry. Capitalism encourages private ownership, an idea that Marx found antithetical. Key components of capitalism include competitive markets, private property, and capital accumulation. Also known as the free market or free enterprise economy, capitalism has been dominant in the Western world. Unlike communism where the state is highly involved in the economy, capitalism leans *laissez-faire*, meaning "let do," a system in which transactions between private individuals and entities are free from government intervention, such as tariffs, subsidies, and regulations.

Communism: Coming from the Latin word "communis," meaning common or universal, communism (largely propagated by Karl Marx and practiced by the Soviet Union in the 20th century) is a political and economic system in which property and resources are collectively owned by a classless society and each person works and is paid according to his or her abilities and needs.

Communist League: An international political party established in June 1847 in London, the Communist League was founded by merging the League of the Just under Karl Schapper and the Communist Correspondence Committee, in which Marx and Engels had great influence. Following the Cologne Communist Trial of 1852, the Communist League was formally disbanded. The First International, also known as the International Workingmen's Association (IWA), in 1864, succeeded the organization.

Enlightenment: An intellectual and philosophical movement in the 1600s and 1700s, the Enlightenment was marked by a rejection of traditional ideas and dominated the intellectual community in Europe in the seventh and 18th centuries. Also known as the Age of Reason, the Enlightenment encouraged the use of reason to achieve knowledge, freedom, and happiness. It was characterized by significant revolutions in science, philosophy, society, theology, and politics and advanced ideals like constitutional government, separation of church and state, liberty, and fraternity. Famous Enlightenment philosophers include Francis Bacon, René Descartes, John Locke, Jean-Jacques Rousseau, David Hume, Adam Smith, and Immanuel Kant.

Fascism: While sometimes defined as the extreme power used by totalitarian dictators, Benito Mussolini, the founder of Fascism, defined the ideology as extremely state-focused, almost to the point of becoming a type of religion (even though Mussolini did not tolerate religion). Fascism wanted three basic tenets:

1. "Everything in the state" (the state was supreme)

2. "Nothing outside the state" (every individual should promote the success of the state)

3. "Nothing against the state" (individuals should not question the state)

Unlike socialism or communism, which emphasize the workers and classes respectively, Fascism emphasizes the state in contrast to the individualism of classical liberalism.

German Confederation: The Congress of Vienna (1814-1815) established the German Confederation, an organization of 39 German states to replace the erstwhile (former) Holy Roman Empire. There was no central executive, so it was a loose political association designed for mutual defense.

Manifesto: A public declaration of the intentions, opinions, or views of the issuer, whether it is an individual, group, political party, or government

Marxist-Leninism: The way in which Vladimir Lenin adapted and interpreted the doctrines of Marx (and Engels) to bring communism to Russia, Marxism-Leninism is the political ideology adopted by the Soviet Union and Comintern as well as Mao Zedong in China. Lenin modified Marx's beliefs that capitalism is a great evil to say that imperialism is the highest form of capitalism and thus should be eradicated. Lenin's book entitled *Imperialism: The Highest Form of Capitalism* published April 1917 is still regarded an important work in the study of imperialism.

MEGA (**Marx-Engels-Gesamtausgabe**): The largest and most complete collection of Marx and Engels's works published in German (or any language for that matter), *MEGA* contains material from Marx between 1838 and 1883 (his death) and from Engels between 1838 and 1895 (his death). The material includes well-known works by Marx, including *The Communist Manifesto* and *Das Kapital* as well as previously unpublished or untranslated works. The project, now overseen by the Internationale Marx-Engels-Stiftung (IMES) since 1990, intends to publish over 110 volumes in order to publish the pair's complete works.

Proletariat: Frequently used in reference to Marxism, proletariats are workers or working class people, often discussed collectively. The term comes from the Latin proletarius, meaning a Roman citizen who owned little or no property. In Marxist theory, proletariat specifically refers to industrial workers who only have their labor as significant material value in contrast to the bourgeois who control the means of production.

Revolutions of 1848: Known also as the Spring of Nations, People's Spring, Springtime of the Peoples, or the Year of Revolution, the Revolutions of 1848 were a series of political upheavals throughout Europe in 1848. It would the most widespread span of revolutions that Europe has ever seen. Essentially democratic in nature, the revolutions began in France in February and spread to most of Europe. Over 50 countries were affected, but the revolutionaries did not collaborate across country lines. The revolutions played the most prominent role in France, the Netherlands, the states that would make up the German Empire after 1871, Italy, and the Austrian Empire. While there was little political change, the revolutions did bring about substantial social and culture change. Their duration was brief. All were suppressed by 1849.

Secularism: The principle of the separation of government institutions from religious institutions, secularism can mean a system of political or social philosophy that rejects all forms of religious faith and worship. Marx believed that religion alienated individuals from society and thus rejected organized religion in his system, arguing instead that materialism is human-focused.

Socialism: While Marx and Engels' *Communist Manifesto* introduced communism as a concept in 1848, socialism was an older idea. Similar to communism, yet different, socialism is an economic and political system in which the government owns and controls the means of production and distribution of goods. It was designed to empower the working class and give them more control. Socialist ideals inspired some to found experimental communities based on egalitarian distribution of wealth and common ownership of resources like land. Many failed within several years.

Totalitarianism: Based on the Italian word "totalitario" meaning complete and absolute, the word totalitarian originated in the early 1900s and refers to a system of government in which only one political party is tolerated and individuals are required to completely obey the state. Indicative of a variety of regimes in the 20th century, including Nazi Germany, Fascist Italy, and Communist Cambodia (the Khmer Rouge under Pol Pot), totalitarianism is a political system that requires absolute control by the state. The government is normally centralized and dictatorial, and attempts to regulate every aspect of public and private life. Hannah Arendt's book *The Origins of Totalitarism*, published in 1951, is the definitive work that analyzes and studies the rise of Nazism and Stalinism, the major totalitarian political movements in the 20th century.

Philosophers and Their Beliefs

Friedrich Engels: Karl Marx's close confidant and friend, Engels co-authored *The Communist Manifesto* with Marx. Based on his observations and research in Manchester, Engels published *The Condition of the Working Class in England* in 1845, which Marx read. He was extremely impressed, leading to the famous meeting of Marx and Engels on August 28, 1844.

Marx and Engels were fast friends after this meeting, regularly collaborating and discussing projects as well as Engels lending Marx money. After Marx's death in 1883, Engels oversaw the publication of Marx's works until Engels's own death in 1895. Unlike Marx, Engels never married, but had a lifelong mistress, Mary Burns.

Georg Wilhelm Friedrich Hegel: A 19th century German philosopher who greatly contributed to Western philosophy, Hegel (1770-1831) influenced a plethora of thinkers, both those who agreed with him and those on the other side. He believed that the *Geist* (Spirit, or sometimes translated Mind) was a historical manifestation and influenced history. In other words, history was always progressing toward the final culmination of Reason. Hegel wanted to defend Kant's dualism of mind and body and bring the two (the infinite and the finite, respectively) together in a self-transcendence. Hegel is known for the concept of the thesis, antithesis, and synthesis although the specific phrase originated with Johann Gottlieb Fichte. *The Phenomenology of Spirit* (or *Mind*) is Hegel's most famous work. Published in 1807, it discusses the progress of consciousness from sense perception to absolute knowledge.

Young Hegelians: After the death of Hegel in 1831, a group of German intellectuals, known was the Young Hegelians or the Left Hegelians, in the decade after his death wrote and responded to his legacy. Some of the Young Hegelians disagreed with Hegel's conclusions, but utilized his dialectical approach, often believing they had brought Hegel's theories to their logical conclusion. Many of them were atheists and socialists and wrote about how Christianity was just a myth. David Strauss, the Bauer brothers (Bruno and Edgar), Max Stirmer, Feuerbach, and Marx himself were the prominent individuals.

Bibliography

Callinicos, Alex. *The Revolutionary Ideas of Karl Marx*. Haymarket Books, 2012, p. 1.

Capper, Charles, and Cristina Giorcelli, editor. *Margaret Fuller: Transatlantic Crossings in a Revolutionary Age*. University of Wisconsin Press, 2008, p. 18.

Carver, Terrell, editor. *The Cambridge Companion to Marx*. Cambridge University Press, 1991, p. 11.

Chapman, J. *The Westminster Review*, vol. 151, Frederick Warne and Company, January-June 1899, pp. 585-6.

Corey, Michael Anthony. *Back to Darwin: The Scientific Case for Deistic Evolution*. Rowman & Littlefield, 1994, p. 12.

Easton, Loyd David and Kurt H. Guddat. *Writings of the Young Marx on Philosophy and Society*. Hackett Publishing Company, 1997, p. 39.

Engels, Friedrich. Preface to the 1888 English Edition of *the Communist Manifesto*. *Marx/Engels Selected Works*, vol. 1, by Karl Marx and Friedrich Engels, Progress Publishers, 1969, p. 9, www.marxists.org/archive/marx/works/download/pdf/Manifesto.pdf. Accessed 13 August 2017.

———. "Speech at the Grave of Karl Marx." Transcribed by Mike Lepore. *Marxists Internet Archive*, 1993, www.marxists.org/archive/marx/works/1883/death/burial.htm. Accessed 17 August 2017.

Furet, François. *Marx and the French Revolution.* University of Chicago Press, 1998, p. xi.

"German Silver Coins." *Hessen*, www.amason.net/hessen/thaler.htm. Accessed 31 July 2017.

"Gymnasium." Encyclopedia Britannica, 20 July 1998, www.britannica.com/topic/Gymnasium-German-school. Accessed 2 August 2017.

Holmes, Rachel. *Eleanor Marx: A Life.* A&C Black, 2014.

Hosfeld, Rolf. *Karl Marx: An Intellectual Biography.* Berghahn Books, 2012, p. 16.

Illingworth, James. "Review of *The Eighteenth Brumaire of Louis Bonaparte.*" *International Socialist Review* 78, July 2011, isreview.org/issue/74/eighteenth-brumaire-louis-bonaparte. Accessed 16 August 2017.

Inge, Sophie. "The things you really need to know about Napoleon." *The Local*, 18 June 2015, www.thelocal.fr/20150618/ten-fascinating-facts-about-napoleon. Accessed 1 July 2017.

"Jenny Marx Longuet (Jennychen)." *Marxists Internet Archive*, www.marxists.org/archive/marx/bio/family/jenny/index.htm. Accessed 30 August 2017.

Johnson, Elliott, David Walker, and Daniel Gray. *Historical Dictionary of Marxism.* 2nd ed. Rowman & Littlefield, 2014, p. 277.

Kamnka, Eugene, editor. *The Portable Karl Marx*. Penguin Group, 1983.

Lenin, Vladimir Ilyich. "Frederick Engels." *Lenin Collected Works* on the Marxists Internet Archive, 1896, p. 15, www.marxists.org/archive/lenin/works/1895/misc/engels-bio.htm. Accessed 12 August 2017.

———. "Speech Delivered in the Name of the R.S.D.L.P. at the Funeral of Paul and Laura Lafargue November 20 (December 3) 1911." *Lenin: Collected Works*, vol. 17, translated by Dora Cox. Progress Publishers, 1974, p. 304-305. www.marxists.org/archive/lenin/works/1911/nov/20.htm. Accessed 31 August 2017.

Levy, Richard, translator. *Gesetz-Sammlung für die Königlichen Preußischen Staaten 1812* [*Collection of Laws for the Royal Prussian States 1812*]. Georg Decker, 1812, pp. 17-22. germanhistorydocs.ghi-dc.org/pdf/eng/15_TheJews_Doc.8English.pdf. Accessed 1 August 2017.

Marx, Karl, and Friedrich Engels. *The Communist Manifesto*. Tribeca Books, 2011.

———. *The German Ideology*. Edited by C.J. Arthur. International Publishers Co., 1972, p. 53.

Mayr, Ernst. "Darwin's Influence on Modern Thought." *Scientific American*, 24 November 2009, www.scientificamerican.com/article/darwins-influence-on-modern-thought/. Accessed 13 August 2017.

McLellan, David. *Karl Marx: A Biography*. 4th ed., Palgrave Macmillan, 2006.

Mehring, Franz. *Karl Marx: The Story of His Life*, vol. 13. Psychology Press, 2003, p. 206.

Mussolini, Benito. "The Doctrine of Fascism." *The Social and Political Doctrines of Contemporary Europe*, edited by Michael Oakeshott, Cambridge University Press, 1939, pp. 164-8.

Nietzsche, Friedrich. *Human, All Too Human I.* Translated by Gary Handwerk. Standford University Press, 1995, p. 63.

Parker, J.W. *The University of Bonn: Its Rise, Progress, & Present State,* West Strand, 1845.

Ryan, Alan. *On Marx: Revolutionary and Utopian.* W.W. Norton & Company, 2014.

Spargo, John. *Karl Marx: His Life and Work.* B.W. Huebsch, 1910, p. 177.

Sperber, Jonathan. *The European Revolutions, 1848-1851.* Cambridge University Press, 1994, p. 152.

————. *Karl Marx: A Nineteenth-Century Life.* Liveright Publishing Corporation, 2013.

Stapley, Pierre. "Marx Becomes a Young Hegelian." Cardiff University, 2010, www.cardiff.ac.uk/socsi/undergraduate/introsoc/marx1.html. Accessed 2 July 2017.

Snyder, Timothy. "Hitler vs. Stalin: Who Killed More?" *The New York Review of Books,* 10 March 2011, www.nybooks.com/articles/2011/03/10/hitler-vs-stalin-who-killed-more/. Accessed 28 August 2017.

Teter, Magda. "Conversion." YIVO Encyclopedia of Jews in Eastern Europe, 2 August 2010, www.yivoencyclopedia.org/article.aspx/Conversion. Accessed 1 August 2017.

Thomas, Mark L. "Marx on the Freedom of the Press." *Socialist Review* 376, January 2013, socialistreview.org.uk/376/marx-freedom-press. Accessed 12 August 2017.

"Trier: The Center of Antiquity in Germany." 8 March 2012. *PDF* file, www.landesmuseum-trier.de/lib/02_Programm/antikencard-trier-englisch-2012.pdf. Accessed 31 July 2017.

Virdee, Satnam. "Socialist antisemitism and its discontents in England, 1884-98." *Patterns of Prejudice*, 20 June 2017, pp. 14-5, dx.doi.org/10.1080/0031322X.2017.1335029. Accessed 1 August 2017.

Wheeler, Brian. "What is Marx's Das Kapital?" *BBC News*, 7 May 2017, www.bbc.com/news/election-2017-39837515. Accessed 28 August 2017.

Wright, Carroll Davidson. *Comparative Wages, Prices, And Cost of Living: (from the Sixteenth Annual Report of the Massachusetts Bureau of Statistics of Labor, for 1885)*. Reprint ed. Wright & Potter Printing Co., 1889, p. 60.

Zou, Shipeng, and Xuegong Yang. *Rethinking Marx*. CRVP, 2007.

About the Author

Rachel Basinger teaches history and other humanities classes to ninth and 12th graders at a small private school in Williamsburg, Virginia. She received a Bachelor's degree in history from Hillsdale College in 2014. Many of the elective classes she took focused on modern history, and she wrote two undergraduate theses on Spanish anarchism and national identity in Spain and France, including in Alsace-Lorraine which had to deal with sometimes conflicting French and Prussian identities just like Karl Marx's Rhineland. A history buff, she loves to study 19th and 20th century history, especially the World Wars and the Cold War.

David MacGregor *at Marx's grave in Highgate Cemetery,*
London. England, on Guy Fawkes Day, Nov. 5,1975.

MacGregor is a professor of sociology at Kings University College, Western University in London, Ontario, Canada.

MacGregor earned his B.A. and M.A. in sociology at Carleton University in Ottawa, the capital of Canada. He spent five years as a sociologist in the Government of Canada. MacGregor won a Canada Council Fellowship (1975-78) and attended the London School of Economics and Political Science in London, England. The University of London recommended his 1978 Ph.D. entitled "Studies in the Concept of Ideology: From the Hegelian Dialectic to Western Marxism" for publication as two books.

MacGregor's first book "The Communist Ideal in Hegel and Marx" (University of Toronto Press, 1984) suggests that Hegel was an even more radical thinker than Marx. "The Communist Ideal" won the John Porter Prize of the Canadian Sociology Association in 1985. Routledge re-published "The Communist Ideal" in 2015 as part of its series, Routledge Library Editions: Marxism.

MacGregor's second book "Hegel, Marx and the English State" (Westview Press, 1992; University of Toronto Press, 1996) examines aristocratic rule, and state intervention against child labor and exploitative factory hours in England in the 19th century. MacGregor contends that Hegel's social and political philosophy inspired Marx's searing indictment of capitalist exploitation in "Chapter Ten: The Working Day" of his magnum opus, "Capital, Volume One."

MacGregor's third book, "Hegel and Marx After the Fall of Communism" (University of Wales Press, 1998; re-published with a new preface and afterword in 2014) presents a balanced discussion of the validity of the arguments of two of the most important political philosophers of all time, Georg Wilhelm Friedrich Hegel and Karl Marx. MacGregor reinterprets Hegel and Marx's philosophies, setting out key episodes in their lives against a backdrop of global historical events. In a new afterword, MacGregor brings his study up-to-date, examining Russia's revival as a world power under Vladimir Putin as well as China's ambitious development efforts.

MacGregor's recent research concerns the astonishing impact of the American Revolution on social and political thought. Conceptualized in MacGregor's proposed fourth book as a series of three civil wars initiated by the bloody struggle between Loyalists and Patriots, the American Revolution spans almost a century from 1775 to the assassination of Lincoln. "The Germans have thought what other nations have done," said Karl Marx. He might well have been talking about the philosopher G.W.F. Hegel and the American Revolution. Perhaps no other thinker has exerted the impact of Hegel on modern thought, and no other event in world history produced such a defining influence on the German philosopher as the American Revolution. The life and work of Hegel form a structuring moment in MacGregor's forthcoming book. Predominant themes in Hegel are also prevailing forces that propelled the New World upheaval: belief in democracy and human rights, opposition to Empire, and the critique of Political Economy.

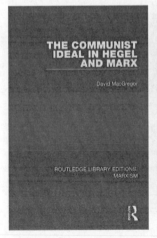

Johan Fornäs is professor of media and communication studies at Södertörn University in Stockholm, the capital of Sweden. He has a mixed and highly interdisciplinary background, having studied mathematics and philosophy as well as musicology. He has conducted research in many fields of media and cultural studies, including work on popular music and youth culture but also more general issues of identity in contemporary society. He lives in Stockholm, Sweden, and in Haut de Cagnes near Nice in southern France.

In the late 1970s, Fornäs organized a series of independent study circles where young adults were introduced to Marx's key work for understanding capitalism: the three volumes of "Capital." For that purpose and context, he wrote a summarizing guidebook, which was later reworked into a book in English: "Capitalism: A Companion to Marx's Economy Critique" (London & New York: Routledge 2013). This pedagogic introduction to Marx's unfinished theory provides a welcome resource for understanding how capitalism works based on how Marx explained the mechanisms of this strange and complex social system. It is a perfect tool for anyone who knows the basics about Marx and his time but wants to be guided into the fascinating universe of his thinking.

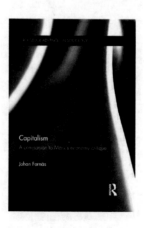

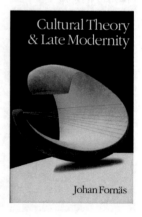

"Consuming Media: Communication, Shopping and Everyday Life" (Oxford & New York: Berg 2007) studies a contemporary shopping mall as a semi-public and commercial urban space of power, profit and communication, focusing on how all sorts of people use all kinds of media.

Fornäs has also published several other books on various topics in media and cultural studies, including "In Garageland: Rock, Youth and Modernity" (London & New York: Routledge 1995), "Youth Culture in Late Modernity" (London: Sage 1995), and "Digital Borderlands: Cultural Studies of Identity and Interactivity on the Internet" (New York: Peter Lang 2002). More recently, two of his books analyze how Europe and European identity is constructed and expressed in different symbols and narratives: "Signifying Europe, and Europe Faces Europe: Narratives from Its Eastern Half" (Bristol: Intellect Press 2012 and 2017).

Finally, a couple of other books serve as introductions to cultural theory and to the concept of culture. They are widely used as handbooks for coming to grips with central ideas on what culture might mean and how it contributes to society, power and identity.

"Cultural Theory and Late Modernity" (London: Sage 1995) overviews a wide range of theories on modernity, power, symbols and identity. The latest one, "Defending Culture: Conceptual Foundations and Contemporary Debate" (Basingstoke & New York: Palgrave Macmillan 2017), distinguishes main definitions of the concept of culture and confronts various post-humanist critiques.

All in all, Fornäs' books offer a wide range of examples of how modern society can be understood through critical theories and analyses in the spirit of Marx, though not limited to his theoretical framework. Readers with a young and open mind can find plenty of fuel for thought in coming to grips with the world of today.

Index